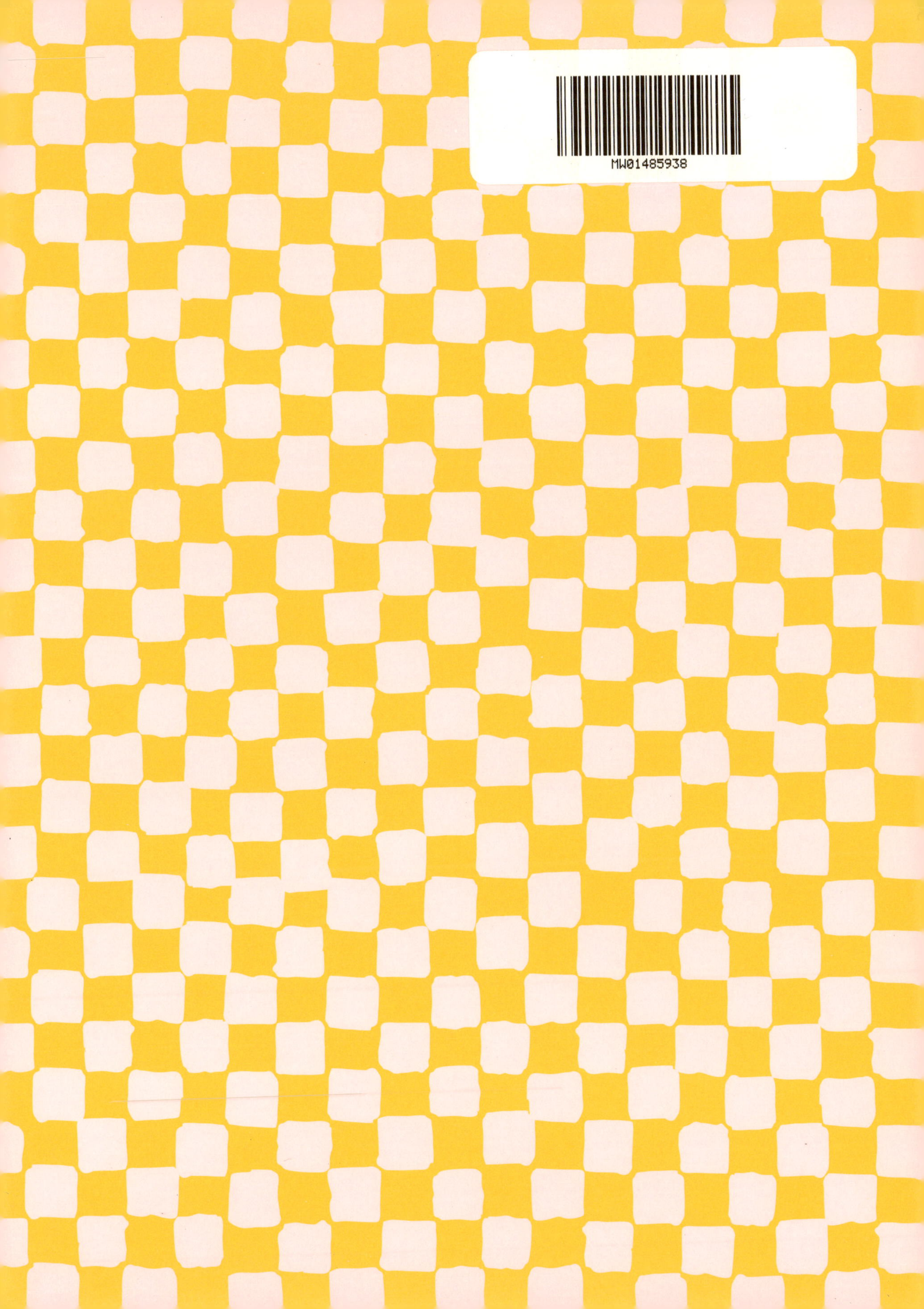
MW01485938

Sugar and spice
and all things nice ...

For my grandmother.
May I always keep biscuits
by my bed in your memory.

By Letitia
Clark

LA VITA È DOLCE

Hardie Grant
BOOKS

Italian-Inspired
Desserts

Preface

While tasting occurs in our head ... it is also part heart.
When the taste is sweet, it triggers a powerful positive response
*in nearly all mammals (cats being the notable exception)**[1]

This much I know: every day of our lives is punctuated by a few distinct highpoints – when we get to eat something. The moments when we get to eat something sweet are often the sweetest moments of all.

Sweet things make us feel happy. Puddings are emotional; soaked in the sweet syrup of nostalgia, scented with fond childhood memories and served with a soft dollop of joyful whimsy. When we are sad it is ice cream, custard, cake and chocolate that we crave, not salads and sardines.

I began writing this book at the very beginning of the Coronavirus pandemic. At home in Sardinia it seemed more important than ever to cling to and celebrate those moments of sweet, everyday pleasure which are – fortunately – available to most. One of the fundamental things about making and eating food, and about making and eating sweet things particularly, is that both actions provide comfort and joy without necessarily being expensive or exclusive. There are not many things in the world that can claim that.

This book is a celebration of Italian-inspired sweet things we can make and eat in our own kitchens, or make and give to others. Baking, by which I mean making cakes, tarts, biscuits and pastries rather than breads, has always been a joyous activity. We bake a cake for a birthday, for Christmas, for Easter, for most festivities, religious or otherwise. An important occasion without a cake to commemorate it seems somehow lacking. Baking is also, by nature, a generous activity. When we make a cake, we are often doing it for someone else. Any and every act of generosity deserves to be celebrated.

Though this book is technically written from an Italian kitchen (specifically a Sardinian kitchen), it is truer to call it Italian-inspired rather than traditionally Italian. The recipes within it are inevitably an eclectic mixture of my experience, my imagination and traditional Italian fare which I have read about, been fortunate enough to have been taught by others, or to have tasted *in situ*. By no means intended to be a complete guide to Italian sweets, as is always the case, the selection reflects my own personal tastes, curiosities and passions, and my own personal preference for speed, ease and glacé cherries.

Most importantly these recipes reflect my own need to find pleasure and joy in the kitchen, and to translate this into simple food that brings pleasure to others. There can be no denying that each day is made infinitely better if we live it in the knowledge that somewhere, tucked away in a cupboard, box or tin, there are some biscuits or a bit of cake.

* My cat loves sweet things.
[1] *The Oxford Companion to Sugar and Sweets*, by Darra Goldstein, Oxford University Press (2015)

Introduction

The Sweet Spot

A steaming bowl of pasta is a very fine thing, but it's the gelato eaten in the dappled sunshine a few hours later which really delights, and in a different way too, because it is a treat. The knowledge that it is something special, a little luxury, an indulgence, not just sustenance (and not necessarily nutrition) makes the pleasure even more poignant. It's not wholesome or satisfying in the same way as savoury food. Instead it thrills, it teases. It's sensual in a way that pasta, pies and potatoes aren't (I'm sure I will receive some indignant emails about the sensuality of potatoes). Whether it's manifested in a velvety-smooth, pale green pistachio gelato, melting onto your hand faster than you can lick it, or an iced dainty in the shape of Venus' breast, nowhere is this sensuality more pronounced than in Italy.

Italians have a sweet tooth to rival my own, and while Italian sweets are sometimes internationally overlooked, there are enough cakes, biscuits and pastries here to keep even the sweetest tooth content. The variety is extraordinary, and of course, as with all Italian food, each region has its own speciality (which is often a very slight variation on another region's speciality).

Interestingly, while savoury Italian food is famed and celebrated for its simplicity and lack of decoration, Italian sweets lean towards the highly decorated, theatrical even. Many of the sweets in Italy provide an elaborate festival of colour, each more shining and glossy than the next, crested with cream and custard, crowned with swathes of meringue and shining strawberries or fluorescent cherries, multicoloured sprinkles and gem-like candied peel. This is because, unlike the majority of savoury dishes, the focus is not on harking back to times of poverty and '*la cucina povera*', but instead a celebration of the arrival of sugar in Italy, introduced by the Arabs and then cultivated in Sicily from as early as the 9th century.

Sweet things have always been inherently playful and nostalgic, both in the way they make us feel and in their very form. They provide the opportunity to be inventive, imaginative and whimsical. This playfulness is nowhere more pronounced than in Italian sweets. Marzipan fruits, cacti made out of sugar, the Sicilian Easter lamb, the infamously Baroque *Cassata* (see p 88), tiny *fruttini* – frozen fruit stuffed with a sorbet made from their own flesh – *dolci* in Italy are a celebration of artistry, of colour, sugar, sensuality and playfulness.

Of course these colourful confections are generally those found in the *pasticcerie*, and those items baked at home tend to be a little more simple or humble. The Italians see no shame in buying their desserts too, and often do not make them at home. When invited for lunch they will habitually give the host a selection of sweets in place of a bunch of flowers. These always come wrapped in pretty paper and tied with ribbons like a gift. Religious festivals, birthdays and other special occasions often prompt *dolci* to be made at home, and for ease and clarity I have highlighted the recipes into the sort of things that you would make/eat every day, and those that you would make/eat for special occasions.

A Sweet Start

'Every dawn is a new beginning, and the day will be what you make of it ... You've got to love a culture that allows you to have ice cream first thing.'

— **A. A. Gill**

To start with a cake, some biscuits or a bun, is without a doubt a day well begun ... Happily for me, breakfast in Italy is rarely savoury. Most often it involves a handful of biscuits or cookies, occasionally some dry toast with jam, almost always washed down with coffee. In the summer, fresh fruit, cold melon slices, perhaps a ripe peach and some yoghurt. As temperatures soar, breakfast may even be a gelato. If having breakfast at a bar, then a sugar-dusted pastry or a *crema*-filled doughnut accompanies the obligatory espresso or cappuccino. These are usually consumed standing, leaning against the bar, the pastry held in a tiny paper napkin, crumbs flying where they will.

Having breakfast '*al bar*' is an experience I still get enormous pleasure from, even after nearly four years in Italy. I love the noise and the ritual of it; the slick skill and studied nonchalance of the baristas, and that sharp, fresh coffee smell mingling with the sweet scent of the false vanilla (which I secretly love) that so many bars use in their pastries. I love that in my favourite place we go to the glass cabinet and choose our own pastries (normally a cream-filled one for me) and then eat them in our crisp paper napkins, side-on at the bar, lifting the tiny, chubby-rimmed coffee cup to our lips to take a hot and bitter sip.

In Italy, a savoury start is mostly viewed with suspicion. I have had lengthy discussions about the infamous full English breakfast – my own national breakfast offering – and some agree it could be good, maybe as a lunch, probably with a beer, but at breakfast – *Che schifo*! Too heavy, too fatty, too meaty, too much. The thought of fried eggs at breakfast – let alone a sausage – usually results in mimed gagging. Baked beans are enough to elicit the sign of the cross.

I've always been a sweet breakfast person, even when I lived in England. It really didn't matter what it was, whether it was technically classified as 'breakfast food' or not; as long as it was sweet I'd have it. Part of the reason I like a sweet breakfast is because it complements the bitterness of coffee, especially if it's (almost painfully) scalding and strong. A sip of bitter black coffee, a bite of something soft and sweet; for me this is the perfect way to start the day. Every day should begin like this; with soft and sweet pleasure, sharpened by a tiny sting of pain.

A Sweet Tooth

I have always had a sweet tooth. It began, as so many stories do, with a grandmother. My granny had a passion for sugar unlike anyone else I've ever known. She would make fresh orange juice for us every morning ('good for us, darlings!') and stir three heaped teaspoons of sugar into her own tiny glass, without which she claimed, it was 'completely undrinkable'. If she served fresh fruit (which she did often) it was doused liberally in sugar, as was her breakfast cereal and everything else. She'd catch me watching her incredulously heap sugar onto her plate, wink at me saucily and say, 'for grit'. Melon slices were sometimes served as a fancy starter, and they too received a liberal inch of the white stuff.

My first introduction to coffee (aged about seven) was a sugar lump that she would place on a teaspoon, bathe briefly in her cup of coffee, then spoon into my open mouth. She called these coffee-soaked sugar cubes – slightly morbidly – 'drowned ducks'. Biscuits were her real weakness. For all the years that I knew her she had beside her pillow a small tin full of biscuits for her own midnight emergencies, or for unexpectedly early mornings, when all of us grandchildren piled into her bed and begged her to read us stories. Her whole life, she was almost never without a 'biccy' within easy arm's reach. My mum, too, eats two ginger biscuits every night before she goes to bed, almost medicinally.

As a child, I was addicted to ice cream, sweets, doughnuts and iced buns, most of all. At cooking school I stole into the classrooms early to raid the fridge and eat the raw sweet pastry dough we'd made the night before (I love raw dough). Working in restaurants, I felt myself drawn to the pastry section, and I was a pastry chef in many of the restaurants I worked in, but I kept on hopping back and forth, between sweet and savoury, because I hated having to choose.

A Sweet Manifesto

Cooking is a process of elimination. We learn what kind of cooks we are by first learning what kind of cooks we are not. You need to learn what kind of cook you are in order to be truly happy in the kitchen.

I am not always a precise cook, or an impeccably neat pastry chef. But that doesn't matter necessarily, because there are many sweet things which are relatively straightforward to make and do not require perfect precision, and thus they are hopefully more accessible to most people, because we are very few of us trained pastry chefs, and we are all of us short of time, space and energy.

I hope there is nothing within these pages that is intimidating or anxiety-inducing. There are no percentages, no hydration levels. Life is stressful enough. I don't open and flick through recipe books to feel crest-fallen; I open and flick through them to feel encouraged and inspired. I want you to walk away from reading this thinking, *I could make that, and I will.*

Recipe books, for me, are almost a form of therapy. Therapy – obviously – should make you feel better. I want this book to do that; to make you feel inspired, not deflated. I want you to feel capable, not confused. Encouraged, not dispirited. Cooking at home should, after all, be comforting.

Cooking should *never* be a drama, a trauma, or something you feel you just can't do. Baking, for some bizarre reason, has so long been described or portrayed as either some sort of divine gift or a hallowed science – something some people can do and some simply can't. As though some people emerge from the womb with the ability to bake perfect muffins and others not: as though there are two types of people in this world, those that can bake and those that can't. Well that's simply not true. Baking is not a divine gift or even a precise science, at least it doesn't have to be. Anyone and everyone – whether self-confessed 'baker' or not – can produce something magnificent.

A Sweet Inheritance

The Arabs revolutionised the whole of European confectionary by introducing the cultivation of sugar cane in the 9th century. Previously most sweet things had been made with honey or *sapa*, a dark syrup made from grape must (which is still used often in Sardinia today). The widespread cultivation of sugar cane, which began in Sicily and gradually spread through the rest of Italy, allowed a whole new type of confection to be created as sugar – unlike honey or *sapa/saba* – had no inherent flavour. Equally, sugar introduced a whole new world of textural possibilities, as it could be made both liquid and solid, both brittle and chewy, and could make things malleable. Many *dolci* made and sold across Italy today (and especially in Sicily) still bear the Arab imprint and often the Arab name too. In the 1500s convents embraced the production of sweets as a source of revenue, and so became fundamental in the evolution of Italian *dolci*. Though there are very few convents left which still make *dolci* to sell, *pasticcerie* have now taken over the work of the nuns, and recreate their classic *dolci* alongside a selection of sweet creations from all over Italy, which bear the stamp of a long string of occupations by Greeks, Romans, Normans, Spanish and French invaders as well as plenty of more contemporary influences (American-style cheesecakes, *Sachertorte* from Vienna, etc.).

A Sweet Something

Whether made at home, bought in a *pasticceria* or eaten in a bar, in Italy, as in most parts of the world, a little something sweet is eaten every day, by almost everyone. It could be a heaped spoon-full of sugar in the early morning or post-lunch espresso, or a cookie or slice of cake for breakfast or *merenda*: there are always opportunities for a moment of sweetness.

In Italy, sugar does not seem to have been tainted by the same 'nutritional' preoccupations as in the UK. Though of course sugar, like all things, should be enjoyed in moderation, I know if I have a sweet breakfast as I always do, I find myself craving sugar less throughout the day.

Denial and abstinence will always have inevitable repercussions. I have a Neapolitan friend, Cecilia, who lives here, and who loves to make *dolci* at home. She's birdlike, with an impossibly tiny, ballerina-like waist, and as she shows me photos on her phone of endless plates of homemade sweets, she always says, with her eyes twinkling,

'You know, Letizia, a little bit of what you like is good for you.'

A Sweet Stroll: The *Passeggiata*

The *passeggiata* is a wonderful thing, so particularly Italian – a leisurely stroll taken in the early evening primarily to socialise or eat a gelato. It is one of my most-loved bits of Italian life, after *colazione al bar* and *aperitivo*. Strolling along the streets in the late afternoon sunlight with an ice cream in hand, contemplating life between licks, and waving as you pass your neighbours/colleagues/friends, is one of the best ways to spend a warm evening. There is a little village near the sea ten minutes from where I live which has three *gelaterie* perfect for this purpose. On a Sunday afternoon this usually quiet village fills with cars as all of Oristano head out for a *passeggiata*. Cones in hand, we walk along the *Lungomare*, looking out at the glittering sea and inhaling deeply, the salt in the air mingling with the creamy gelato melting in our mouths.

Authenticity and Tradition

I wrote in my first book, *Bitter Honey*, that authenticity in recipe writing is a slippery concept, and this statement is equally relevant here. The wealth of both tradition and traditional recipes in Italian culture is one of the factors that contribute to it being so endlessly fascinating, and one of the reasons it has been written about by so many for so long. This being said, there are those that would argue that a cohesive concept of some sort of 'Italian cuisine' is fundamentally misleading, as Italy became a unified nation only relatively recently. Each region has its own fiercely regional identity and thus its proclaimed authentic regional dishes and traditions, but even then, the lines blur, the broth grows cloudy, and one region's *zeppole* becomes another's *zippole*.

As a French-trained Englishwoman living in Italy (Sardinia specifically) both I and the recipes I cook are inevitably products of my experience and my situation. One of the reasons I love Italian food so passionately is for this infinite variety and regionality, and for the abundance of tradition which contributes to each dish being imbued with meaning and seasoned with both stories and history. What I love most of all, however, is the ethos that lies at the heart of the cuisine – a generosity (even with limited ingredients/budget) and passion that takes simple ingredients and treats them with ingenuity, wisdom, creativity and respect to produce delicious and satisfying food. The recipes included in this book do – I hope – reflect that ethos, whilst they are not all strictly authentically Italian – they take inspiration from both this attitude and the ingredients and combinations that I have encountered here.

The way we cook is informed by the lives we have led: the experiences we have had, the places we have been, the people we have known, the food others have cooked for us. More significantly, the way we cook and eat is forever in evolution. Each cook creates their own traditions in their own home. It may be one Italian family's tradition to add yoghurt to their *Torta di Mele* (see p 107), another's to add cinnamon. Which is more authentic, more traditional, more Italian? And who decides?

When we cook we are creating a home; an imagined one, a remembered one, a real and present one. Cooking connects us both to our past and our present, and to each other. The immigrant's dilemma is to feel forever split slightly in two, right down the middle like a cream bun. The food we cook to fill that gap – the gap between the old home and the new one - like the cream we plaster inside the bun – is something all its own, something which unifies without becoming part of; something simultaneously different but connected. One of the things which has helped me to feel at home here in Italy is recognising those things which are edible echoes of the things I know from my home in the UK. The Roman buns eaten at Lent (*Maritozzi,* see p 168) which remind me of Hot Cross Buns, or the *Sbriciolata* (see p 66) which makes me think of an English Crumble. It is reassuring to think that whatever our differences, culinary or otherwise, we are always united by more than divides us. This is a great source of comfort, inside the kitchen and out of it.

History is written and lived by people and not machines, and people invent, evolve, change and adapt. This extraordinarily messy diversity is something to be celebrated and embraced, both in the kitchen and in life.

Before you Start

Check the Notes on Ingredients on pages 245–250. The recipes were tested using a non-fan oven; reduce the temperature by 20°C (50°F) if using a fan-assisted oven.

PASTICCERIA
Heineken

PIAZZA
PIETRO MARTINI
PRATZA
DE SANTU DOMINIGU

1

BISCUITS

Biscotti

The variety of biscuits made and sold across Italy is extraordinary. Given the widespread culture of eating biscuits for breakfast, for *merenda* (snacks), at festivals and celebrations, or even as a dessert (more specifically as *dolci,* sweets), it is little wonder that such a rich selection is available, and one of the satisfying similarities between the English and the Italians is their communal love of biscuits.

The word *biscotti* derives from the Latin word *biscotus,* meaning 'twice cooked'. The *Cantucci*, or *Cantuccini*, on pages 27 and 28 are the best and most literal demonstration of this description, as they are cooked once whole, and then sliced and cooked again. Traditionally this method of cooking was devised as preservation, as anything twice baked would keep for much longer, as opposed to cakes, which would become stale quickly.

More importantly, however, it means that biscuits are the perfect accompaniment, the crunchy half of a perfect pairing – the dry ying to a liquid yang. The same perfect pairing of crunchy and liquid as that of crisps and beer, or crisps and Campari.

A biscuit lifted, dunked and held, just long enough to be bathed but not so long that it collapses – pieces plopping into the cup with a sad splash – is a simple, everyday thing, but also truly wonderful when you think about it. So cheap to make and to buy, so keep-able, so dunk-able, so portable, so satisfying. The majority of biscuits in Italy revolve around ingredients that are prolific and/or local; nuts, citrus and sugar. Occasionally, if the biscuits are designed for special occasions, they will be spiced or include dried fruit, and unlike the majority of British biscuits they do not always contain copious quantities of butter. However, the Semolina Shortbread on page 44 is a nod to both Italian and British baking traditions.

It would be all-too-easy to write an entire book on *biscotti*, and such books do, I'm sure, already exist. Instead I have picked a handful of those I really love, which occupy a significant place in my heart, for whatever reason.

Tiny Peach & Almond Cookies with Ricotta Cream

There is something irresistibly appealing about these blushing little almond cookies shaped and painted to look like peaches and filled with ricotta cream. I love a culinary *trompe l'oeil*, and I've seen and coveted these often in pastry shops in many parts of Italy. They're perhaps not the sort of thing you'd make every day, as they are a little fiddly (though not complicated), but, much like macaroons, they are exquisitely beautiful, dainty and feminine. They would be the perfect thing to make as a gift, or for birthdays, parties or weddings.

The traditional method of blushing the peaches pink is to paint them with Alchermes, a vivid scarlet Italian liqueur flavoured with a mixture of spices including nutmeg, cinnamon and vanilla, which originally derived its colour from scale insects called Kermes. Modern production leaves out the insects, though it's a drink that still divides opinion, and though many traditional southern Italian *dolci* include it I have offered some alternatives. To accentuate the ground almonds (almond meal) in the cookie dough, I like to paint the cookies with Amaretto, which has a less divisive flavour, combined with a splash of Alchermes for colour and the slightest spicy background note.

I fill my peaches with ricotta cream, though there are many other variations. Sometimes they are filled with apricot (or peach) jam, sometimes with pastry cream (see p 232). Often – as the cherry on the *trompe l'oeil* cake – the cookies are then stuffed with a whole almond to replicate the peach stone.

continued →

continued →

Makes 12–14 sandwiched cookies

For the biscuits

80 g (3 oz) butter
1 egg
80 g (3 oz/⅓ cup) sugar
80 ml (2½ fl oz/5 tbsp) milk
a pinch of salt
finely grated zest of 1 large lemon
170 g (6 oz/1⅓ cups) 00 or plain (all-purpose) flour
1 tsp baking powder
100 g (3½ oz/1 cup) ground almonds (almond meal)

For the filling

250 g (9 oz) ricotta
50 g (2 oz/¼ cup) sugar
½ tsp vanilla extract
12–14 whole almonds (optional)

To decorate

100 ml (3½ fl oz/scant ½ cup) Amaretto
red food colouring or a splash of Alchermes
4 tbsp sugar
mint leaves or fresh lemon verbena leaves

For the biscuits, melt the butter in a saucepan and set aside to cool slightly. Briefly whisk the egg and sugar in a mixing bowl to dissolve the sugar. Whisk in the melted butter and the milk, then add the salt and lemon zest followed by the flour, baking powder and ground almonds. The batter will seem relatively loose – halfway between cookie and cake, but that's fine. Allow it to rest for 5 minutes or so.

Preheat the oven to 180°C (350°F/Gas 4). Line a shallow baking tray (pan) with baking parchment.

Pinch off 24-26 teaspoon sized pieces of dough and roll them into smooth balls between the palms of your hands.

Place the balls on the prepared baking sheet a few inches apart and press them very slightly to flatten.

Bake the cookies for around 12 minutes, or until they still look pale on top but are golden underneath.

Allow them to cool while you make the filling.

Whisk the ricotta in a bowl with the sugar and vanilla extract until smooth and creamy (the sugar will dissolve as you whisk).

Using a sharp knife, cut a small hole in the base of each cookie.

Spoon the ricotta mixture into the holes. If using the almonds, press them into the filling before sandwiching the cookies together. Smooth away any excess ricotta from the edges.

Pour the Amaretto into a bowl and add the Alchermes or food colouring to create a red tint. Pour the sugar onto a shallow plate.

Dunk the cookies briefly in the alcohol, turning them to make sure they are covered all over. (If you prefer you can apply the alcohol with a pastry brush, which will allow the cookies to stay crisper for longer.) Dip and roll them in the sugar, to replicate the downy skin of a peach, and then place a mint or lemon verbena leaf in each.

Serve, with pride.

Note

These will keep for a day or two in the fridge, and will soften slightly because of the alcohol, but are none the worse for it.

Classic *Cantucci*
Orange, Marsala & Almond Biscuits

Cantuccio is an old Italian word that means 'little place', 'nook' or 'corner', often used to describe a piece of bread with a lot of crust, like the corners cut from the end of the loaf. The nub – as I have always known it – is my favourite part of the loaf and I am always happy to receive this often-discarded bit as I love the chewy, almost-burnt crust even more than the crumb. I love how evocative Italian food names can be, and there could not be a better way of describing the shape of these biscuits, which are slightly angular and crust-heavy, in the best possible way. A delicious and sweet little nook in which to seek solace.

A traditional biscuit from Prato, in Tuscany, I assumed, like so many iconic Italian *dolci*, that they would be difficult to make, but they aren't at all. Instead, they are very satisfying and straightforward. The flavour is wonderfully sweet and pure, the texture perfectly crisp, and when eaten alongside a chilled glass of Vin Santo wine they make a very simple but delightful finish to a meal. Of course, they also make a nicely nutty breakfast (the almonds add some vague suggestion of nutrition) with a coffee (cappuccino for a change).

Makes 14

100 g (3½ oz) blanched almonds
30 g (1 oz) butter
2 eggs, plus 1 (beaten), to glaze
170 g (6 oz/¾ cup) sugar
zest of 1 orange
1 tbsp Marsala
280 g (10 oz) 00 or plain (all-purpose) flour
pinch of salt
1 tsp baking powder

Preheat the oven to 170°C (340°F/Gas 3).

Arrange the almonds over the base of a baking sheet and pop them in the oven for 8–10 minutes until lightly toasted. Set aside to cool.

Melt the butter in a small saucepan or in the microwave.

Break the eggs into a mixing bowl and whisk them well with the sugar, orange zest and Marsala. Add the melted butter and whisk to incorporate.

Add the flour, salt, baking powder and toasted almonds and mix together to form a dough. Work the dough with your hands to bring it together.

Turn the oven temperature up to 180°C (350°F/Gas 4) and shape the dough into two logs about 5–6 cm (2½ in) wide.

Put the logs on a baking sheet lined with baking parchment. Brush them with the beaten egg to glaze.

Bake in the oven for 20 minutes, until just golden.

Remove the biscuits from the oven and allow to cool slightly, then cut the logs at a 45-degree angle into slices about 1–2 cm (½–¾ in) wide.

Return the biscuits to the oven for a further 15 minutes or until crunchy and golden.

Remove from the oven and eat with sweet wine, or coffee.

These keep well in an airtight container.

Dark Chocolate, Chestnut & Hazelnut *Cantucci*

One of the things that has been introduced into my baking repertoire since I moved to Italy is chestnut flour, which I love. It has a wonderfully sweet, slightly smoky flavour that adds a whole new level to baked goods. It tastes of bonfires and autumn walks in the woods, and pairs brilliantly with the rich bitterness of dark chocolate.

Makes around 20

100 g (3½ oz) blanched hazelnuts
30 g (1 oz) butter
2 eggs, plus 1 (beaten), to glaze
160 g (5½ oz/¾ cup) sugar
1 tbsp Marsala
200 g (7 oz/2¼ cups) chestnut flour
100 g (3½ oz/¾ cup, plus 2 tbsp) 00 or plain (all-purpose) flour
pinch of salt
1 tsp baking powder
50 g (2 oz) dark chocolate, broken into small pieces

Preheat the oven to 170°C (340°F/Gas 3).

Arrange the hazelnuts over the base of a baking sheet and pop them into the oven for around 10 minutes, or until lightly toasted. Set aside to cool. Roughly chop them into large pieces using a sharp knife.

Melt the butter in a small saucepan or in the microwave.

Break the eggs into a mixing bowl and whisk them well with the sugar and Marsala. Add the melted butter and whisk to incorporate.

Add the flours, salt, baking powder, chocolate pieces and toasted, chopped hazelnuts and mix together to form a dough. Work the dough with your hands to bring it together.

Turn the oven up to 180°C (350°F/Gas 4) and shape the dough into two logs about 5–7 cm (2 in) wide.

Put the logs onto a baking sheet lined with baking parchment. Brush with beaten egg to glaze.

Bake in the oven for 20 minutes, or until just golden.

Remove the biscuits from the oven and allow to cool for around 15 minutes (this is quite a crumbly dough and the biscuits will keep their shape better if sliced when a little cooler). Using a long, sharp knife, cut (don't saw or they will crumble) the logs at a 45-degree angle into slices 1–2 cm (½–¾ in) wide.

Return the biscuits to the oven for another 15–20 minutes, or until crunchy and golden.

Remove from the oven and eat with a glass of sweet wine, or coffee.

Capigliette

Another product of a convent, and one of Sardinia's most beautiful and unique *dolci*, these little almond tartlets are traditional for celebratory occasions such as baptisms and weddings. They are found all over the island, and referred to by various names. In the south they are known as *Pastissus*, and near Oristano as *Capigliette*.

Made in special small, fluted, tin moulds (see note, overleaf) they consist of a paper-thin pastry case filled with a light, lemon-scented almond sponge mixture, and topped with a simple icing glaze. They are then intricately decorated with sugar icing (royal icing known as *ghiaccia reale*), which is piped with exquisite delicacy to create lace-like patterns. Occasionally this icing may then be crusted with gold leaf or embellished with silver balls or tiny iced flowers.

This quantity makes enough for a *festa*, or special event, which is realistically the most likely occasion you will want to make these, as they do take time and are relatively involved and fiddly – the sort of things that women in a Sardinian family or village will come together and spend the entire day making. However, the sight of a whole tray of their intricately decorated and delicate white beauty is truly memorable, and well worth the effort involved.

Makes around 20 small (two-bite size) tarts

For the pastry

165 g (5½ oz/1⅓ cups) 00 or plain (all-purpose) flour, plus extra for dusting
pinch of salt
25 g (¾ oz) lard or butter, plus extra for greasing
70 ml (2½ fl oz/5 tbsp) water

For the filling

3 eggs, separated
100 g (3½ oz/½ cup) sugar
finely grated zest of 1 large lemon
1 tbsp orange blossom water
165 g (5½ oz/⅔ cup) ground almonds (almond meal)

For the *ghiaccia reale*

220 g (8 oz/1¾ cups) icing (confectioner's) sugar
40 g (1½ oz) egg white (1 medium/large egg white)

For the pastry

Put the flour, salt and lard or butter in a mixing bowl and rub in the fat using your fingertips until the mixture resembles fine breadcrumbs. Add the water and bring together with your hands to form a smooth dough. (If using a mixer, you can put all the ingredients together and mix until smooth.)

Remove the dough from the bowl and transfer to a clean work surface. Knead the dough well for at least 5 minutes, until smooth and silky. (You can make the dough in a stand mixer with a dough hook attached, if you wish.)

Wrap the dough in clingfilm (plastic wrap) and set it aside to rest for at least 30 minutes.

Using a pasta machine, or a rolling pin if you don't have one, roll out the dough until it is very thin (about 1 mm), aiming for the same thinness as if you were making ravioli. It should be just thin enough that it's becoming transparent when you hold it up. You may need to use a sprinkling of flour to stop the dough from sticking.

Lightly grease the tin moulds with melted butter and put the rolled pastry inside, trimming up the edges to fit.

continued →

continued →

For the filling

Preheat the oven to 170°C (340°F/Gas 3).

Whisk the egg yolks with half of the sugar in a mixing bowl until you have a fluffy, mousse-like consistency. The mixture should at least double in size. Add the lemon zest, the orange blossom water and the ground almonds and fold gently to incorporate.

In a separate mixing bowl, whisk the egg whites with the remaining sugar until the mixture forms soft and glossy peaks. Fold the whites into the egg yolk and almond mixture, stirring gently to incorporate everything without losing too much air.

Use a teaspoon to transfer the mixture into the prepared pastry cases. The filling will rise significantly on baking so only fill the cases about two-thirds full. Smooth the sponge mixture to make a flat top.

Place the tartlets on a baking tray and then put them in the oven. Cook for around 15 minutes, until the tops of the sponge are golden brown and the pastry only just beginning to take a little colour.

Remove from the oven and allow to cool.

For the *ghiaccia reale*

Gently mix the icing sugar and egg white in a bowl until they come together to form a smooth glaze.

Delicately paint the top of the tarts with this glaze, or dip them upside-down into the glaze and wipe away any excess. Make sure you get a good even covering over the surface, right to the edges; any excess will drip away. Reserve the icing that is left in the bowl.

Allow the glaze to dry completely.

Meanwhile, whisk the reserved icing using an electric whisk or beater attachment on a stand mixer. Whisk well for a few minutes until the icing is opaque and white, like meringue. It should be shiny and white and much thicker than previously. Make a tiny piping bag with a piece of greaseproof (waxed) paper (or use a disposable piping bag, just cutting the tiniest tip off to create a very small hole) and decant some of the royal icing into it. Cut the tip off to create a tiny nozzle and then gently pipe patterns onto the top of the tartlets. Allow the icing to set.

It is good to practise your patterns a little on some baking parchment first, before piping them directly onto the tarts – this way there is room for trial and error.

Notes

As is always the case, the lard in the pastry means that the finished texture is wonderfully crisp, but if you prefer to use butter, then you can substitute an equal amount.

The moulds are available online and from cook shops, sold as small tartlet tins. If you cannot find the special moulds you can use small, shallow muffin tins, like those you would use for jam tarts, small quiche moulds, or moulds used for Portuguese custard tarts and use a fluted cutter to cut the pastry bases. I have made them this way before and they work well.

Little Jam Flower Cookies

These little jammy flower-shaped cookies, called *Ciambelline*, are enormously popular in Sardinia, and with good reason. They're lovely to look at, quick to make and popular with everyone. They are also the perfect thing to make with children (if you make them with children, filling them with Nutella rather than jam seems to be the most popular option, unsurprisingly).

If you make your own jam, then of course use that. The recipe for Apricot Jam on page 242 is a favourite. (Seedless) raspberry jam is good, as is a crab apple jelly or blackberry/blackcurrant jam. Anything a little bit tart. Like most Sardinian *dolci*, these are traditionally made with lard, but you can replace it with butter. The dough can be frozen easily and used at a later date.

You can make these with simple round cutters if you can't find flower-shaped ones, or any other shape you like (such as stars for Christmas), but it's nice to have the hole in the top part of the cookie so you can see the shiny, jewel-like jam through it, like a Jammy Dodger.

Makes 30–40

500 g (1 lb 2 oz/4 cups) 00 or plain (all-purpose) flour
175 g (6 oz/1⅓ cups, plus 2 tbsp) icing (confectioner's) sugar, plus extra for dusting
pinch of salt
1 tsp baking powder
200 g (7 oz) butter or lard, softened
1 whole egg and 1 egg yolk
1 tsp vanilla extract
zest of 1 lemon
1 jar of your favourite jam or Nutella

Mix all the ingredients together in a stand mixer until you have a smooth dough. (If making it by hand, put all the dry ingredients into a mixing bowl, add the butter or lard and rub the fat into the dry ingredients until the mixture resembles breadcrumbs. Mix in the egg and egg yolk along with the vanilla and lemon zest, kneading gently until you have a smooth dough.)

Wrap the dough in clingfilm (plastic wrap) and put in the fridge to rest for 30 minutes.

Preheat the oven to 170°C (340°F/Gas 3). Line two large baking sheets with baking parchment.

Remove the chilled dough and roll it out to a 2–3 mm (⅛ in) thickness. Use your cutters to cut equal numbers of top and bottom pieces. Carefully lift the cookies onto their baking sheets and space them 1 cm (½ in) or so apart.

Transfer the sheets to the oven and bake until just golden, 15–18 minutes. Allow to cool before placing a teaspoon of jam or Nutella onto each base, and then placing the top cookie over it and pressing down gently.

Dust with icing sugar and serve.

These keep well in an airtight container for up to 4 days.

Amaretti

Many times here in Sardinia I have been offered a small, innocuous-looking little oblong biscuit at a party or after Sunday lunch, taken a bite and felt my teeth sink gently into the sweet, almondy chew of a good *Amaretto*. Though they look unassuming, their texture and flavour are totally beguiling, so much so that I assumed they must be difficult to make, or at least that there must be some special knack or trick to them.

I couldn't have been more wrong. They are one of the simplest things imaginable. My wonderfully impatient but gifted friend, Loredana, showed me how to make them. Everything can be done in a few minutes, by hand. No whisking, beating, creaming necessary. The ingredients list couldn't be shorter or simpler.

Deriving their name from *amaro* (bitter), *Amaretti* (little bitter ones) are small, baked biscuits made using a combination of sweet and bitter almonds. They are found all over Italy, in various shapes and guises, though those known most abroad come from Saronno in Lombardy, and are sold wrapped in crisp white paper printed with blue calligraphy and presented in beautifully ornate tins.

Bitter almonds contain chemical compounds, chiefly amygdalin, which breaks down when exposed to moisture into benzaldehyde and hydrogen cyanide (which is poisonous). Both of these compounds contribute to the distinctive scent of bitter almonds (which you will also recognise as the same scent as Amaretto Disaronno liqueur, Bakewell tarts, almond essence and maraschino cherries). Most bitter almonds are in fact the kernels of stone fruits, specifically peaches and apricots. If you use a few drops of almond extract instead of bitter almonds, then use the full 500 g (1lb 2 oz) of standard almonds.

Makes about 30

460 g (1 lb) blanched almonds
40 g (1½ oz) bitter almonds or 1 tsp almond extract
400 g (14 oz/2 cups) caster (superfine) sugar
140 g (4½ oz) egg white (see note on p 37)
2 tbsp icing (confectioner's) sugar, to sprinkle

Grind both types of almonds with the sugar in a blender until you have a fine powder.

Stir the egg whites with a fork to mix them a little. If using almond essence, add it with the egg white.

Tip the ground almonds into a bowl and add the egg whites, little by little, bringing the dough together to form one sticky mass. The dough needs to be able to hold its shape, and should be sufficiently dry that it doesn't stick to your fingers, but not so dry that it feels sandy.

Preheat the oven to 170°C (340°F/Gas 3). Line a large baking sheet with baking parchment.

Wetting your hands slightly, take golf-ball or large walnut-sized balls of dough and roll them into even-sized sausage shapes. Placing the sausages lengthways in the palm of your hand, press an index

finger in the centre to create a domed top, then lay them (indent-side down) on a baking sheet lined with baking parchment.

When you have shaped all of the dough, brush the tops of the *Amaretti* with any remaining remnants of egg white and sprinkle with the icing sugar (this gives them a shiny crust).

Bake in the oven until golden and brown, about 13–15 minutes. Allow to cool, or eat while still warm and extra chewy.

As these are at their best when chewy, keep an eye on them as they cook, and taste one to check they are still soft.

These freeze well, and will keep in a tightly sealed container for up to 2 weeks.

Ricciolini
Chewy Lemon & Almond Biscuits

For those who hate the taste of bitter almonds, there are *Ricciolini*; sweet and simple, soft almond biscuits made from a pure paste of standard almonds, egg white and sugar. The finely grated zest of a good lemon is added, and the flavour is light, sweet and lemony. Their texture, like the ones on page 34, is the perfect blend of chewy and crunchy. My friend Loredana, whose recipe this is, usually pipes these with a fluted nozzle, to make little swirls or hedgehog shapes, hence their name (*riccio* means 'hedgehog' in Italian), but if you prefer you can shape them into balls or rounds or any other form you like. These are usually topped with half a glacé (candied) cherry or a whole unblanched almond.

Makes about 30

500 g (1 lb 2 oz) blanched almonds
400 g (14 oz/1¾ cups) caster (superfine) sugar
zest of 1 lemon
140 g (4½ oz) egg white
glacé (candied) cherries, halved or whole almonds, to decorate

Grind the almonds, sugar and lemon zest into a fine powder in a blender. Transfer to a bowl and add the egg white, little by little, until you have a soft dough.

Preheat the oven to 180°C (350°F/Gas 4). Line a large baking sheet with baking parchment.

If piping, scoop the mixture into a piping bag (you will need a strong fabric one here, rather than a disposable plastic one) and pipe little swirls about the size of a golf ball onto the baking parchment. (Loredana disposes with the bag and pushes balls of the mixture straight through a thick nozzle using her hands.) If shaping by hand, wet your hands slightly, roll small golf-ball sized pieces and then flatten them slightly into rounds with the palm of your hand once they're on the baking parchment.

Press half a glacé cherry or whole almond into the top of each, transfer to the oven and bake for 13–15 minutes, until golden brown but still chewy.

Note

For either of the previous recipes you can buy ground almonds (almond meal) if you prefer, but the consistency and flavour will differ slightly and Loredana will be displeased.

MOKA

In the bar we drink espresso. At home we make moka. Moka coffee is to many Italians the greatest coffee of them all. To some Italians, it is the only coffee.

Making a moka is an art. An art which I was taught by a very patient perfectionist who had first been taught by his nonna when he was 6 years old, and who has done it the same slow, specific way every day of his life since that day. A lot of experience, some patience and a pinch of precision, but a sure-fire method that yields perfect results.

To make a moka you need a moka pot. The most widely distributed brand is Bialetti. There are many other makes on the market, but I love the little Bialetti man with his handlebar moustache, pinstriped trousers and perky pointing finger. The Little Man with the Moustache, as he is officially known, is in fact Mr Alfonso Bialetti himself, the creator of the very first moka pot back in 1933. The name moka comes from the city of Mocha on the Red Sea coast of Yemen, one of the first and most important areas of coffee production. The moka pot has remained unchanged since its invention. It comes in a range of sizes, from a single cup to 9-cups' worth. If you can find the single-cup one, I advise you to buy it, if only for purely sentimental reasons. It is impossibly dinky.

Once you have your pot, you fill the water container with cold water, just up to the point where the screw is. Then you fill the funnel part with as much (espresso-ground) coffee as you comfortably can, until it forms a slightly peaked powder mountain. Don't press it down as this changes the flavour (so the moka mystics say). Now gently screw on the top part and place the whole thing on the smallest hob.

After a few unhurried minutes, anticipation brewing, the telltale smell of freshly brewed coffee hits your nostrils and you sigh inwardly with relief. You lift the cap and see a thick brown liquid bubbling up through the spout. Turn the heat down to low. Leave the moka brewing on a low heat until all of the coffee has bubbled up, then remove from the heat and set aside for a minute. Stir the coffee with a teaspoon, then pour it carefully into your chosen cup.

'What would life be without coffee?
But then, what is life, even with coffee?'

— **King Louis XV of France**

In terms of flavour, moka coffee should be strong, bracingly so, but it should never taste burnt in the way espresso can. Drinking moka coffee is refreshing in a way that espresso isn't; it's much more a drink to be lingered over. An espresso is a short, sharp slap in the face, a jolt to the system, an assault on the senses. You leave the restaurant/bar and stumble into the street feeling at first dizzy, then determined. Moka, however, can be a little more lingering, a little more luxurious. It allows you time to think and to savour.

For me, both have their place and their pleasures.

The ritual of making the moka is one I have become extremely attached to since moving to Italy. I used to resent it – the time it took, the delicate handling and concentration needed to not scatter coffee grounds everywhere. Now I enjoy it. It provides a welcome pause first thing, forcing me to slow down and concentrate on a simple task in hand.

Making a moka every morning as I do means that I am always left with a little coffee, as I habitually make the 4-cup, and then drink only half. The other two cups go into a jar in the fridge. When I want to make *tiramisù* or coffee granita, I then have the coffee ready. If I want to drink iced coffee on a hot July day, then I have some ready-made coffee in the fridge; I just add ice and sometimes a splash of cold milk.

Pabassinus
Spiced Grape Must, Raisin & Nut Cookies

These little diamond-shaped biscuits are found all over Sardinia, with recipes differing from region to region. *Pabassinus*, deriving their name from the Sardinian word *pabassa,* which means 'raisin', are traditionally made for All Saints' Day (1 November), the addition of spices, citrus zest and a large quantity of dried fruit and nuts being the edible markers of religious festivals. Crumbly, nutty and wonderfully spicy, they are so inseparable from the period leading up to *Ognissanti* that when I asked a friend if she would make them with me in September, she point-blank refused. I first made these with a friend's aunt, who measured everything by eye ('*quanto basta!*') and baked them in a wood-fired oven as she had done on the same day every year for her entire life. Many households in Sardinia still have these ovens, which are lit for special occasions. Traditionally bread is baked first, then, as the temperature cools, the *dolci* are baked afterwards.

Saba, or *sapa* is a dark, richly flavoured syrup made from cooked grape must. Traditionally in Sardinia this was also made from prickly pears (*fichi d'India*), which grow wild all over the countryside. They were gathered with canes and then boiled down with water to produce a thick, dusky syrup which was then used as a sweetener. Few people make this syrup now, but sapa made from grapes is still used for many traditional *dolci*. If you can't find sapa, then a dark honey, black treacle or date molasses are all good substitutes.

The biscuits are usually decorated with a simple white glacé icing and multi-coloured sprinkles (Sardinians are inordinately fond of sprinkles) but they are also very good un-iced and unsprinkled. They keep well in an airtight container for a few days.

Makes 30 larger or 40 smaller cookies – enough for a *festa*

100 g (3½ oz) blanched almonds
70 g (2½ oz) walnuts
2 tsp aniseed
120 g (4 oz) raisins

Preheat the oven to 180°C (350°F/Gas 4). Arrange the almonds over the base of a baking tray (pan) and roast in the oven until just lightly golden, about 8–10 minutes.

Remove from the oven and chop the almonds lengthways into nibs. Chop the walnuts roughly.

Toast the aniseed in a dry shallow pan for 1–2 minutes or until it begins to smell good. Remove and bash the seeds gently in a pestle and mortar, or in a deep bowl using the bottom of a rolling pin.

Soak the raisins in boiling water (or tea or coffee or anything hot you have to hand – fennel tea would also be nice) until softened (around 3 minutes). Drain them well in a sieve, squeezing to remove any excess liquid.

270 g (10 oz/2¼ cups) 00 or plain (all-purpose) flour, plus extra to dust
140 g (4½ oz/2⅔ cups) sugar
120 g (4 oz) butter or lard, at room temperature
1 egg and 1 egg yolk
½ tsp salt
1 tsp baking powder
pinch of cinnamon
pinch of ground cloves (optional)
1 tbsp sapa
zest of 1 lemon
zest of 1 orange

For the icing

130 g (4 oz/1 cup) icing (confectioner's) sugar
2 tbsp lemon juice (juice of 1 lemon, roughly)
sprinkles (optional)

In a bowl, mix together the chopped nuts, bashed aniseed and soaked raisins with the rest of the ingredients using your hands (messy but satisfying) or using a wooden spoon until you have a smooth dough. Wrap the dough in clingfilm (plastic wrap) and leave to rest in the fridge while you clean up.

Once the dough has rested for 30 minutes, roll it out on a work surface dusted with flour. Roll out to 1 cm (½ in) thickness, then cut diagonally into large-ish diamond shapes, rerolling and cutting any edges until you have used all of the dough.

Place on a baking sheet lined with baking parchment and bake for 12–15 minutes (keep a close eye on them as they burn fast). Remove and leave to cool.

To make the icing, mix the icing sugar with the lemon juice in a small bowl until just at pouring consistency.

Decorate the biscuits with the icing and sprinkles, if using.

Note

These are almost always made into rough diagonals here in Sardinia, but if you prefer to use your favourite cookie cutter then feel free to do so. They'd make very good Christmas cookies too.

Semolina Shortbread

Good shortbread – by which I mean buttery, friable, golden and sweet biscuits that melt in the mouth – has won a place in Italy's fastidious culinary heart. When discussing the relative merits and demerits of traditional English foods (something I do surprisingly frequently) one thing that is accepted as a given is our ability to produce the most delicious buttery biscuits. Shortbread is one of the simplest things in the world, and one of the most delicious when done well. It is also a celebration of butter, which is one of my favourite ingredients. The addition of *semola* (see p 247) is both a nod to Italy and a clever way of enhancing the crumbliness of the texture. The best shortbread recipe I have ever found, and a happy culinary meeting of English and Italian minds.

I am lazy about shaping shortbread, as I usually serve it in rough shards alongside the posset on page 126. This way you simply roll it out into a rough, single piece of even thickness, bake it and then snap it into uneven pieces afterwards. However, if you wish to shape it into a sausage, chill it and slice it and then bake it in neat rounds, you can do this.

Makes 12 pieces

- 175 g (6 oz) butter, at room temperature
- 90 g (3 oz/¾ cup) icing (confectioner's) sugar
- ½ tsp salt
- 75 g (2½ oz/⅔ cup) semolina or semola
- 175 g (6 oz/1⅓ cups) 00 or plain (all-purpose) flour

In a stand mixer (or mixing bowl using an electric mixer), beat the butter and icing sugar until pale and fluffy. Add the salt, semolina and flour and mix briefly until the dough comes together.

(If making by hand, put the dry ingredients into a mixing bowl, rub in the butter as if making a crumble, then mix together until you have a dough.)

Remove the dough from the bowl (the bowl – and your hands – should be perfectly clean). Wrap it in clingfilm (plastic wrap) and leave to chill in the fridge for 25 minutes.

Preheat the oven to 160°C (320°F/Gas 2).

Roll the shortbread out onto a piece of baking parchment to a 3–4 mm (⅛–¼ in) thickness.

Place the piece of baking parchment (with the shortbread on it) on a baking sheet and bake in the oven for 30–40 minutes, until golden all over. Allow to cool before eating.

HOTEL GRANDE BRETAGNE-LAMPSA
ATHÈNES

Cubana

2

TARTS

Crostate

Tarts in Italy are known as *crostate*. Although they're a little more fiddly and time-consuming to make than cakes, tarts are wonderful, and work both as breakfast and as puddings. They are also excellent as an indulgent *merenda* (snack).

The fiddliest part of making tarts is blind baking the pastry base, a step that is not difficult once you get the hang of it, but adds to the total prep time. One way to save time is to make your pastry in advance and store it in the freezer; you can also line tart shells and store them ready to be baked (if your freezer allows you enough space to do this).

There are some tarts, like the *Crostata di Marmellata* on page 50, that do not require the blind-baking of the base, and thus can be achieved very quickly and easily (it is also a traditional and very good breakfast tart).

Crostata di Marmellata

Crostata is the grown-up, enlarged, Italian cousin of a jam tart. Usually eaten at breakfast, with a small, strong coffee, it satisfies the breakfast jam craving, and also the flaky buttery craving that anyone who enjoys toast with butter and jam, or a buttery croissant with jam (everyone, surely) feels when they wake up and take their first sip of bitter black brew.

The *crostata* is well-known and loved all over Italy, including here in Sardinia. As a typical *dolce* which many still make at home, it is often very rustic in shape and form, and is not something you necessarily need to fuss over. The crust, after which it is named, *crosta* meaning 'crust', can be as thick as you like it, to an extent. My friend's Nonna, who was a famously irritable and impatient (but simultaneously very gifted) cook, made her crust an inch thick, because she liked it like that, and she pressed it roughly into place with impatient hands, perennially scratched from rose-pruning, rather than rolling it out thinly. So feel free to be carefree. It is, after all, your crust.

The pastry of a *crostata* is usually a simple *pasta frolla*, a sweet butter-and-egg pastry dough. Occasionally a teaspoon of baking powder is added to the dough, which makes the *crostata* even more cakey, though I prefer it without. As this is a simple, homely sort of thing, it makes sense that the pastry is so too. This, like the jam tarts of my childhood, is a wonderfully easy and satisfying thing to make with children.

Serves 12

- 1 × quantity Sweet Pastry II (see p 236)
- 1 jar (280 g/10 oz) of your best jam
- 1 egg white, beaten, to glaze

Make the sweet pastry according to the instructions on page 236.

Use a 23 cm (9 in) metal tart tin with removable base or a fluted ceramic pie dish (see note, opposite). Roll out the pastry (you can simply press it into place in the tin, which is also fine) to 3–4 mm (⅛–¼ in) thickness and line the tart shell. Trim off the excess and save it for the lattice top. You may need to use a sprinkling of extra flour on your work surface and rolling pin if the pastry starts sticking, depending on the temperature of the room.

Place the pastry-lined tart tin in the fridge to chill, then roll out the excess pastry and cut (using either a pastry cutter for crinkly edges or a knife for straight ones) into strips for the lattice top. You may need to move these in and out of the fridge depending on how warm they get, so roll and cut them straight onto a piece of baking parchment so you can move them about easily.

When the pastry shell has chilled (after 10 minutes or so) spread the base with the jam. Arrange the lattice strips on top, pressing the edges well into the dough to seal. Brush the lattice with egg white then return the tin to the fridge for another rest.

Preheat the oven to 190°C (375°F/Gas 5).

Bake the tart in the oven for 20–25 minutes, until golden brown.

Note

This is one of the few pastry tarts you don't have to blind-bake, which makes it all the more lovable and, because the jam is not too liquid-heavy the bottom stays nice and crumbly and dry, without any sogginess in sight.

I usually make this in a simple, old-fashioned, fluted ceramic pie dish, so that you don't even need to worry about turning it out of the tin, just slice it straight from the dish.

Caramelised Citrus Tart

This is a lovely tart. The base is buttery, biscuity and crisp, and the curd is sharp and sassy. The filling involves no faffing about with cream or milk: just pure, unadulterated citrus tartness lubricated by the silkiness of butter. A filling that wobbles just as much as your upper thigh.

Grilling it may sound odd, but it ensures the filling stays that almost-impossible, just-set silkiness, like lemony Vaseline, and still has the delicious flavour of caramelisation. Those patches of brown where the citrus and sugar have caught, those are corner-of-the-lasagne, sticky-bit-at-the-bottom-of-the-pan gold.

This filling can easily be made into jars of citrus curd that work well as gifts (to yourself or otherwise). This is my perfect citrus curd mix, but you can choose to make it pure lemon or otherwise. Add bergamot if you're lucky enough to find it, or Seville orange in January (substitute 50 ml/3 tbsp of lemon juice for bergamot or Seville – this is equivalent to about 1 fruit so use the zest of that fruit also) or blood orange when in season (this will also add a lovely pinky hue to it).

Serves 10–12

For the pastry case

Prepare and blind bake the pastry case using a 30 cm (12 in) tart tin by following the recipe and method for Sweet Pastry II (see p 236)

For the filling

3 whole eggs
5 egg yolks
250 g (9 oz/1 cup, plus 2 tbsp) sugar
finely grated zest and juice of 4 lemons
finely grated zest and juice of 3 clementines
finely grated zest and juice of 1 small orange (all of the citrus juice should come to 300 ml/ 10 fl oz/1¼ cups in total)
200 g (7 oz) butter, cut into pieces and at room temperature

Have your prepared pastry case ready and have to hand a sieve set over a large, deep bowl.

Preheat the grill to maximum heat.

For the filling, in a bowl, mix the eggs and yolks with the sugar and the citrus zest and juice, then transfer to a heavy-based saucepan over a low heat. Whisk gently until all the sugar melts. Add half the butter and turn the heat up to medium, whisking constantly. The mixture should begin to thicken after a few minutes, at which point add the rest of the butter a piece at a time, whisking continuously. If things are catching and the mixture looks like it might curdle, turn the heat down to low again. Once the mixture has reached the consistency of a loose custard (after about 10 minutes of cooking and stirring) and small bubbles are just beginning to appear at the edges, quickly pour it through the sieve and into the bowl.

Transfer the mixture to the prepared pastry case, put the tart on a baking sheet and place it delicately under the grill. Leave the door open and watch as the top of the tart bubbles, burnishes and browns. This should take 10–15 minutes, depending on the heat of your grill. Remove the tart when you are happy with the colour (check it still has a nice wobble in the centre (see Cooking until 'baveuse', p 257).

The filling may look loose, but will firm up after chilling. Allow to cool *completely* before serving. This tart can be kept in the fridge for a few days.

Note

The grilling method will only work properly if you use a wide tart shell with a low 2 cm (¾ in) rim, otherwise the top of the pastry case will catch under the grill. The case should be almost flush with the filling. If your tart tin is deeper and thus so is your pastry shell, ignore the grilling method and bake the tart instead in a preheated oven at 170°C (340°F/ Gas 3) oven for 8–10 minutes, until the filling is just set. Allow to cool to room temperature before refrigerating and serving cold.

Chocolate & Mascarpone Tart with Blackberries & Sage

This is a lot less complicated than it may initially seem, and is a lovely thing to make and eat in late summer/early autumn. The pairing of blackberries and sage is an inspired one; the sage adds a musky, citrus edge to the wine-flavoured berries. The chocolate pastry looks wonderfully striking against the black berries, and the filling is merely a question of a quick whisking (no cooking of custards).

Serves 10–12

For the tart shell

Prepare and blind-bake the pastry case using a 28 cm (10 in) tart tin with removable base, following the recipe for Chocolate Pastry (see p 236)

For the mascarpone filling

3 tbsp icing (confectioner's) sugar
zest and juice of 1 lemon
400 g (14 oz) mascarpone

For the blackberries

400 g (14 oz) blackberries
zest and juice of 1 lemon
50 g (2 oz) sugar
60 ml (4 tbsp) water
6 sage leaves

Optional extra

Crystallised Sage Leaves (see p 260)

For the filling, mix the icing sugar with the lemon zest and juice in a large mixing bowl. Stir in the mascarpone and keep the mixture chilled until you need to use it.

For the blackberries, purée/blitz/mash half of the blackberries (reserve the other half for decorating the tart).

Cook the mashed berries in a small saucepan with the lemon zest, sugar, water and sage leaves. Simmer gently for 10 minutes, or until thick and jammy.

Set aside and leave to cool. Remove and discard the sage leaves. Stir in most of the lemon juice and taste, adding more if it needs more sharpness.

Once ready to assemble your tart, spread the mascarpone mix evenly over the chilled pastry base.

Spread over the cooled blackberry jam purée, then arrange the remaining berries over the top. Decorate with a few crystallised sage leaves, if using.

Note

This is also very good decorated with sliced fresh figs rather than blackberries.

Fig & Red Wine *Crostata*

This is really a riff on a French *galette* masquerading as a *crostata*, but if you have an abundance of good, ripe fruit it begs to be made into all kinds of tarts from all pockets and corners of Europe and beyond. In England this pastry would be known as a type of rough puff pastry because the method of keeping large flakes of butter entire in the dough gives it a crumbly, flaky, layered texture.

One of the best ways to eat fruit is to bake it in an open tart such as this one. The fruit cooks to jammy sweet-sharpness, and the crisp, burnished pastry crust provides the perfect foil. The pastry has only a very little sugar in it, as most of the sweetness should be provided by the fruit. The crust instead acts as a pure, buttery, flaky contrast to the syrupy fruit it encases.

It is, thankfully, much less work than real puff pastry, and is only achievable by hand, and very therapeutic to make.

If you prefer to use simple white sugar, you can. I like the toffee sweetness of Demerara here.

Serves 6–8

For the dough

200 g (7 oz/1⅔ cups) 00 or plain (all-purpose) flour
pinch of salt
160 g (5½ oz) butter, cubed
2 tbsp Demerara sugar (1 for the dough and 1 to sprinkle at the end)
1 tsp lemon juice
50 ml (4 tbsp) iced water
1 egg, beaten, to glaze

For the fig filling

500 g (1 lb 2 oz) fresh figs, topped and quartered lengthways
50 ml (4 tbsp) red wine
2 tbsp Demerara sugar

For the dough, put the flour and salt in a large mixing bowl. Add the cubes of butter and toss them in the flour with your fingers, making sure they are all coated. Begin to press them into flat discs in your fingers and keeping tossing as you do so to make sure they stay coated in flour. Once all the butter cubes are now flakes, and are well distributed through the flour, add 1 tablespoon of sugar and the lemon juice and water. Bring the dough together with your hands (if it still looks too dry and flaky add a touch more cold water). It is quite a rough dough, so do not aim for smooth and shiny, but it needs to come together in one clean piece with no dry bits at all.

Pat the dough into a round, wrap it in clingfilm (plastic wrap) and leave it to chill for at least 40 minutes in the fridge or freezer.

When ready to assemble the tart, roll out the pastry to 3–4 mm (⅛–¼ in) thickness (this is quite a rustic tart and the pastry is nice if it's quite thick).

For the fig filling, put the fig quarters in a bowl and toss them with the wine and sugar. Leave to macerate for a few minutes.

Preheat the oven to 180°C (350°F/Gas 4).

Put the rolled pastry on a flat baking sheet lined with baking parchment. Arrange the figs over the centre of the pastry, leaving a 2.5 cm (1 in) border.

Fold the edges of the pastry on themselves to create a rough round crust.

Brush the pastry edges with beaten egg (optional but gives a good shine) and sprinkle with the remaining tablespoon of sugar. Bake the crostata for around 45 minutes, or until the filling is brown and bubbling. Serve with a blob of cold mascarpone or ricotta ice cream.

Note

This is also very good with peaches, pears or plums, or any late summer/early autumn fruit. Just make sure you taste the sweetness of your fruit and adjust the amount of sugar you add to it.

Note

You can make this in a 23 cm (9 in) crostata tin, which is halfway between a pie dish and a cake tin, with 2–3 inch sides, or in a 23 cm (9 in) spring-form cake tin.

Pastiera Napoletana

Good things come to those who wait.

Traditionally, *Pastiera Napoletana* would have taken the entire week preceding Easter to prepare. Hailing originally from Naples, and a symbolic celebration of spring and new life, it was probably born in a convent like so many classic Italian *dolci*. The elaborate ritual of preparation made the final eating on Easter Sunday that much more special. Like so many festive *dolci*, this is a project, but a pleasurable one. I've narrowed down the process here to about four days. However arduous the process may initially seem, this finished tart is truly worth the wait. The ritual of beginning something in anticipation of a final feast on Easter day is enormously rewarding.

Hard to describe to those that do not already know it, this tart is utterly unique and not a little eccentric. It's a sort of orange-and-spice scented ricotta cheesecake baked in a sweet pastry case and topped with a pastry lattice. The thing that makes it really unusual, though, is that the filling is flecked with plump little cooked wheat grains (berries). The combination is addictively delicious, and this tart has won itself somewhat of a cult following.

The candied fruit in the filling is traditionally *cedro* (citron), so use that if you can find it, otherwise candied orange is a good option. If you can find ready-cooked farro, known as *grano cotto* (see p 247), and available in some Italian supermarkets, then this will make your life much easier.

Serves 8–10

3 days before baking

Soak 100 g (3½ oz) farro or wheat grains (berries) in plenty of cold water, changing the water daily, for three days.

For the pastry

500 g (1 lb 2 oz/4 cups) 00 or plain (all-purpose) flour, plus extra for dusting
200 g (7 oz/1⅔ cups) icing (confectioner's) sugar
pinch of salt
zest of 1 orange
250 g (9 oz) butter, plus extra for greasing
5 egg yolks, plus 1 egg (beaten) for the egg wash to finish

For the pastry, put the flour, icing sugar, salt, orange zest and butter in a food processor and blitz to a fine breadcrumb consistency. Add the egg yolks to the mixer and blend again briefly, until the mixture comes together as a dough (add a tablespoon or two of iced water if the dough is still dry and does not come together). Form the dough into two equal rounds with your hands. Wrap in clingfilm (plastic wrap) and chill in the fridge or freezer, depending on when you want to use it. It needs to rest for at least 30 minutes in the fridge before you roll it.

Grease a deep 23 cm (9 in) cake tin/crostata tin with butter, then dust it lightly with flour. After the dough has rested, roll it out to a rough 2 mm (1⁄16 in) thickness and line the cake tin, pushing the dough up the sides of the tin to create a 5–7.5 cm (2–3 in) depth and trimming any overhang. Don't worry too much about perfectly thin, even pastry. Reserve the pastry trimmings for the lattice top. Chill the pastry case in the fridge for 30 minutes.

Preheat the oven to 180°C (350°F/Gas 4).

Remove the pastry case from the fridge and blind-bake (see p 236 for more about blind baking). Allow to cool while you prepare the filling.

continued →

continued →

For the farro or wheat berries

100 g (3½ oz) soaked farro or wheat grains (berries)
350 ml (12 fl oz/1½ cups) milk
1 cinnamon stick
zest of 1 lemon
pinch of salt

For the rest of the filling

350 g (12 oz) ricotta
4 egg yolks
zest of 2 oranges
100 g (3½ oz) finely chopped candied orange or *cedro* (citron)
250 g (9 oz/1¼ cups) sugar
1 tbsp orange blossom water
½ tsp vanilla extract or the seeds from ½ vanilla pod (bean)
pinch of salt
3 egg whites

For the farro or wheat berries, on the third day of soaking, drain the soaked grain. Cook in a saucepan with the milk, cinnamon, lemon zest and salt over a very low heat, covered with a lid. Cook, stirring occasionally for 30–40 minutes until the grain is plump and tender and all the milk had been absorbed. Spread the grain out on a plate to cool completely.

Preheat the oven to 170°C (340°F/Gas 3).

For the rest of the filling, whisk or beat the ricotta in a bowl until smooth, then whisk in the egg yolks. Stir in the orange zest, candied fruit, sugar, orange blossom water, vanilla and salt. Into this mixture, stir the cooled cooked wheat. In a separate bowl whisk the egg whites to soft peaks, then fold them gently into the ricotta mixture.

Pour the whole lot into the prepared pastry case. Cut the leftover pastry dough into strips about 2 cm (¾ in) wide, and arrange them over the top in a diagonal lattice. Use your fingers to press the edges of each strip into the pastry case walls to seal them.

Brush the top of the tart with the beaten egg and bake for 90 minutes, or until biscuit brown all over.

Let the tart cool and the filling settle, for at least 12 hours in a cool place before slicing into it.

Serve, finally, with coffee and congratulations.

Roasted Apricot, Almond, Orange & Mascarpone Cheesecake

Cheesecake – unbaked and with a biscuit base and a cream cheese filling, has, for some or other reason, been happily assimilated into Italian food culture.

Whether wholly traditional or not, this is a lovely arrangement: fresher, lighter, juicier than a baked version, and with a good buttery biscuit crust. The roasted apricots are a minimum-effort, maximum-effect addition.

Serves 8–10

For the base

100 g (3½ oz) butter, melted
pinch of salt
250 g (9 oz) biscuits (I use ginger ones)

For the filling

250 g (9 oz) cream
250 g (9 oz) mascarpone
50 g (2 oz) icing (confectioner's) sugar
zest of 1 orange
zest of 1 lemon, plus 1 tsp of the juice

For the topping

300 g (10½ oz) fresh apricots
1 tbsp Amaretto (optional)
3 tbsp sugar
30 g (1 oz) flaked almonds

Grease and line a 23 cm (9 in) spring-form cake tin.

To make the base, break the biscuits however you see fit (blitzing in a food processor or bashing with a rolling pin) and mix them in a bowl with the melted butter and salt. Press the mixture into the base of the cake tin, then chill in the fridge.

Preheat the oven to 180°C (350°F/Gas 4). Bake the base for 10–15 minutes, until a deeper shade of brown and toasty-smelling. Remove and allow to cool.

For the filling, whip the cream to soft peaks. Gently fold in the mascarpone, sugar, citrus juice and zest, and set aside. Once the base is cool spread over the cream mixture. Chill in the fridge until ready to serve.

For the topping, turn the oven up to 200°C (400°F/Gas 6). Halve the apricots, remove and discard the stones and place the halves in an ovenproof dish cut-side up, then roast for 15–20 minutes until they begin to take colour. Sprinkle over the Amaretto (if using) and the sugar and scatter the flaked almonds over the top. Roast for another 10 minutes, or until the almonds are golden and the apricots are juicy and bubbling. Allow to cool, or serve hot on top of your cheesecake. Either is good.

Ricotta & Dark Chocolate Almond Crumble Tart *Sbriciolata*

This is a hybrid of a cake, a crumble, a giant cookie, a tart and a biscuit. Technically not quite any of them, but with delicious echoes of all of them. I like these sort of unclassifiable recipes: there should always be anomalies in life, it makes it that much more interesting. If I really had to describe it in one pithy phrase, I would say it is a giant crumble pie.

Sbriciolata, which means 'crumbled', deriving from the verb S*briciolare*, to crumble or create crumbs, is one of the various names given to this *dolce* which hails originally from Lombardy but pops up regularly all over Italy. *La Sbrisolona*, a traditional crumble-cake from Mantua, seems to be the original from which all other variations derived, and was made using a combination of lard, hazelnuts and polenta, a much simpler and more humble version and a product of the *cucina povera*. Over the years it has changed and evolved in both name and components. This is my favourite version.

I admit I stumbled upon it in my quest to discover an Italian equivalent of my favourite English pudding, the infamous crumble. Though this is not really the same, there are many satisfactory nostalgic reverberations. The addition of polenta to the crumb is presumably a nod to the tart's northern origins, and while many modern versions do not include it, I like the texture it gives, a sort of pleasing sandiness. The same is true of the almonds.

Best eaten with a coffee for breakfast, or mid-afternoon, it keeps well for a few days – in the fridge is best because of the ricotta. The method of making the pastry/dough is much like the method of making English crumble, working everything in your fingers into a loose and ragged rubble. I find this soothing, and as irregularity is part of the charm here, this is one of the rare occasions where I never use a machine. If you want to save time, you can ignore me and use a machine.

Serves 8–10

For the crumble

100 g (3½ oz) whole blanched almonds or 100 g (3½ oz/1 cup) ground almonds (almond meal)
170 g (6 oz/1⅔ cups) 00 or plain (all-purpose) flour
100 g (3½ oz/⅔ cup) polenta
150 g (5 oz) butter, cut into rough chunks
pinch of salt
150 g (5 oz/⅔ cup) sugar
2 egg yolks
lemon zest (optional)

For the filling

500 g (1 lb 2 oz) ricotta (pour off any excess liquid, but no need to drain)
70 g (2½ oz/½ cup) icing (confectioner's) sugar
70 g (2½ oz) dark chocolate, broken, blitzed or cut roughly into shards

Preheat the oven to 180°C (350°F/Gas 4). Grease and line a 23 cm (9 in) cake tin.

For the crumble, grind the almonds in a processor (if using ground almonds, omit this step). Put all the remaining ingredients for the crumble into a large bowl and work the mixture between your fingers as if you were making pastry. When the mixture is evenly mixed and you have a bowlful of scraggy crumbs, cover the bowl and place it in the fridge to chill.

For the filling, mix the ricotta with the icing sugar in a bowl and whisk it well until smooth and creamy. Mix the chocolate shards into the ricotta and stir until the cream is evenly flecked with chocolate pieces.

Remove the chilled crumble mix from the fridge. Press half of it into the base of the prepared cake tin to form an even base layer with a slightly raised edge to contain the ricotta mixture.

Spread the ricotta and chocolate mixture over the base, smoothing it out to form an even layer.

Sprinkle the remaining crumble mixture over the top to cover evenly (you shouldn't see any of the ricotta mix at all, only crumble).

Transfer to the oven and bake for 40–50 minutes, or until golden brown all over. Remove and leave to cool. I like this best eaten straight from the fridge, when firm. It keeps well for a few days.

recipe photo overleaf →

Note

If you want to make this as a plain crumble cake, without a filling (in which case it is much more like a giant cookie, but none the worse for it), then it is a nice addition to add the zest of a lemon to the crumble mix. If you want to change the filling, you can add almost anything. Try jam, lemon curd or chopped fresh fruit.

Sunny Sardinian Citrus & Ricotta Tartlets

These little tartlets (*Pardulas/Formagelle/Casadinas*), always perfumed with citrus and occasionally also with saffron, are a traditional sweet made all over Sardinia during Easter. The ingredients differ slightly between regions – in some villages it's traditional to add honey, in others raisins. Their name too varies depending on where you are. Their sun-like shape, however, is universal, as is the inclusion of ricotta and citrus: two of Sardinia's signature ingredients.

With a fluffy, almost cheesecake filling, and a simple crisp pastry base, these are so delicately sunny and unassuming that you can easily polish off a whole plateful without really thinking about it. Because they are shaped by hand and involve sprinkles, they are a great thing to make (and eat) with kids. Sprinkles make everything better.

Flavourings can be vanilla, saffron, orange blossom water. I like to use a combination of vanilla and orange blossom water. They are not overly sweet, and for extra sweetness you can top them how you like – I have given a few different options (see p 73).

A pasta machine is useful.

Makes 16–20 small tarts

For the pastry

30 g (1 oz) lard or butter
200 g (7 oz/1⅔ cups) semola (finely ground durum wheat flour; see p 247)
100 g (3½ oz/¾ cup, plus 2 tbsp) 00 or plain (all-purpose) flour
120 ml (4 fl oz/½ cup) warm water
pinch of salt

For the filling

2 egg yolks
zest of 1 orange and 1 lemon
70 g (2½ oz/⅓ cup) sugar
500 g (1 lb 2 oz) ricotta, drained well
1 tsp orange blossom water (optional)
½ tsp of vanilla extract
pinch of salt
60 g (2 oz/½ cup) 00 or plain (all-purpose) flour

Line 2 baking sheets with baking parchment.

Make the pastry. In a bowl, rub the lard or butter into the semola and flour with your fingertips until the mixture resembles fine breadcrumbs. Add the water and salt and knead well to form a smooth dough. You will need to knead for a good 10 minutes or so.

Wrap the dough in clingfilm (plastic wrap) and allow to rest for at least an hour.

Using a pasta machine (or rolling pin), roll out the pastry to around a 2 mm thickness. Cut 16–20 circles (using a pastry cutter or upturned glass of your choice) and place on the prepared baking sheets. Re-roll the trimmings as needed and try to use up all the pastry.

Preheat the oven to 170°C (340°F/Gas 3).

For the filling, mix the egg yolks with the citrus zests and sugar in a bowl and beat well. Add the ricotta along with the orange blossom water, vanilla and salt, and mix well until you have a smooth paste. Add the flour and mix again to form a smooth batter. Spoon the mixture into the centre of each pastry round and pinch the edges of the pastry to form a star/sun shape. Smooth the tops using the back of a wet teaspoon, or a wet finger.

Bake in the oven for 10–15 minutes, until golden. Top each tartlet according to preference (see options overleaf).

These are better if eaten a few hours later, after the flavours have settled.

Options to finish

Lemon Glaze Icing (see p 238)
Lemon Glaze Icing and sprinkles
Citrus syrup (simply boil the juice of 1 large lemon with 30 g/1 oz sugar in a small pan, stirring, until a syrup is formed)
Warmed honey, drizzled over

Sylvia's Double-Crusted Cheesecake

A genius invention by my friend Sylvia, who took the *sbriciolona* idea a step further and made a sort of giant cheesecake sandwich with it.

Everybody knows that the best bit of a cheesecake is the biscuit, just like the best bit of a crumble is the crumble. Everybody also knows, however, that the only way to appreciate the biscuit base is to have something tangy and creamy against it, otherwise it would just be a biscuit. Crumble without the sharp fruit under-bit to contrast against its sweet, buttery-biscuity-ness would seem equally incongruous. But the eternal dilemma of any obsessive such as myself is how to create more crust without compromising on cream? Here, Sylvia has answered all our prayers and created a double-crust, crumble-cheesecake-sandwich. We can have our cheesecake, and eat it too.

The filling is simple, a mixture of sweetened Philadelphia cream cheese and mascarpone lifted with a little lemon zest. Folded through the cream filling can be any fruit of your choice, whatever is in season and appealing. I like raspberries and peaches best, as a sort of peach melba tribute. To decorate (as the top is simply a smooth biscuit layer) you can use a tumble of surplus fresh fruit, or leave it plain and unassuming, so that people are even more pleasantly surprised when they realise how delicious it is.

Sylvia uses a combination of oat biscuits and digestives, which works very well, but you can use pure digestives or pure oat biscuits if you prefer.

Serves 12

For the crumb

380 g (13½ oz) biscuits, crushed into crumbs
160 g (5½ oz) butter, melted
pinch of salt

For the filling

250 g (9 oz) full-fat Philadelphia cream cheese
400 g (14 oz) mascarpone
zest and juice of 2 lemons
100 g (3½ oz/¾ cup) icing (confectioner's) sugar
150 g (5 oz) peaches/raspberries/blackberries (or fruit of your choice)

Preheat the oven to 160°C (320°F/Gas 2).

To make the crumb, crush the biscuits in a food processor or by hand and put in a bowl. Pour the melted butter over the crushed biscuits, add the salt and mix well.

Grease and line a 23 cm (9 in) spring-form cake tin. Press half of the crumb mixture into the base to form an even layer, pressing down with the underside of a spoon or the base of a glass tumbler to make a compact, even base.

Transfer to the oven to bake for 10–15 minutes (this initial baking ensures the crust stays crisp and biscuity rather than soggy once it has the cream mixture on top).

Set aside to cool completely. (Keep the oven on.)

For the filling, put the cream cheese and mascarpone in a bowl, then mix in the lemon zest and icing sugar until smooth and incorporated. Prepare your chosen fruit (if using peaches, chop them into slices or chunks and macerate with the lemon juice; if using berries simply stir them with the lemon juice).

Strain off the excess lemon juice, then gently stir the prepared fruit through the cream mixture and spread it out evenly over the

cold crumb base. Spread the remaining half of the crumb base over the top and smooth it over with the back of a spoon to form an even layer.

Bake the cheesecake in the oven for 12–15 minutes, or until the biscuit has turned a shade darker. Remove and allow to cool completely, then chill in the fridge before serving.

Serve unadorned, or with extra fruit as you see fit.

This keeps well in the fridge for a few days and is very good for breakfast.

RICOTTA

Ricotta is a magical thing. It is endlessly versatile, equally good in sweet and savoury dishes, and capable of being both ethereally light *and* cheesily rich.

Just-made ricotta (*ricotta appena fatta*), if you get the chance to taste it, is delicate, sweet and light; a little lactic whisper that disappears on the tongue almost immediately. Fresh, warm ricotta, eaten straight from the vessel in which it was made, is something many Italians feel very romantic about. It's an echo of childhood and edible evidence of alchemy.

Chicco, our local cheesemaker, speaks in hushed tones as he hands a teaspoon to each of us to taste. I have stood around a great cauldron-like pot like this many times, always in a group of habitually loud, burly Sardinian men, who crowd closer and fall strangely silent when it comes to tasting a spoonful. For me, it provides an echo of my English childhood – Little Miss Muffet, her curds and whey, and the junket my granny used to make for us as a treat.

Samuel Lai makes his ricotta with local sheep's milk. The sheep are milked by hand, and Samuel collects the milk and uses it to make his cheeses. Ricotta is a by-product of the cheese-making process, a way of using what's left behind to create something that is arguably even more valuable and more versatile than the original product.

Samuel uses the initial curds to make pecorino, then adds some fresh milk to the remaining whey, heating it gently (*ricotta* means 're-cooked') until the liquid reaches around 75°C (165°F). At this point the proteins in the whey begin to coagulate. Cloudlike curds swarm in the translucent yellow liquid, collecting in droves like flocks of sheep in a storm. These delicate, wobbling curds are gently lifted out and ladled into traditional reed baskets, any remaining whey seeping away slowly over time.

For many people, the truest ricotta is made from sheep's milk. Because of the proliferation of sheep in Sardinia and the large amount of sheep's cheese produced here, it is easy to buy fresh sheep's milk ricotta. Compared to cow's milk ricotta,

it is simultaneously richer and much more delicate, with a more sheepy, complex flavour.

I still enjoy cow's milk ricotta, and use and buy both depending on what is available. Most of the industrially produced ricotta is made from cow's milk, and the tubs you find in supermarkets usually contain pasteurised cow's milk ricotta, made from milk rather than from whey. It has a smooth, uniform texture, and is still good and useful in the kitchen – and because it is pasteurised, it lasts longer than the fresh, fleeting stuff too.

For the real experience, however, it is worth seeking out, even if only once, the real thing straight from the source.

Ricotta in the kitchen

One of the most amazing things about real, unpasteurised, fresh ricotta is how it changes over time. It continues to lose liquid (this is why ricotta is almost always sold in plastic baskets, sitting in a puddle of pale yellow whey), so its texture changes, becoming denser and more creamy/cheesy by the minute. The first day you taste it, the texture will be different from the third day, for example, and this is one of the capricious joys of fresh ricotta versus the homogenous nature of the stuff in tubs.

Ricotta is a wonderful and essential addition to the baking storecupboard. Used in cakes and tarts it provides a cheesy richness and moistness. It adds a bounce to the crumb of cakes, a creaminess to pancakes, and a fluffiness to everything.

I realise it is not always easy to find good, fresh ricotta so I have tried to make allowances for this in the recipes. There are some recipes in which the flavour and texture of the ricotta itself is an essential element in the finished dish. Many of the classic Sicilian *dolci*, – *Cannoli* and *Cassata* for example – rely on good-quality ricotta as it is a key ingredient, the main event rather than a background note. If making these sorts of *dolci*, it is important to source good-quality ricotta.

When using ricotta as an ingredient in cakes, tarts or crumbles, it is fine to use the pasteurised tub version. For certain recipes it is also essential that the ricotta is drained beforehand, so that extra liquid does not affect the finished result.

Torta della Nonna

I have never met anyone that didn't fall in love with this tart, *subito*. It is the edible equivalent of being enveloped in the flowery-bloused bosom of your beloved grandmother/*nonna*. The flavours are simple, creamy, uncomplicated and enormously soothing.

Originally from Tuscany but disseminated all over Italy and equally loved here in Sardinia, this glorious cake/pie/tart is a classic Sunday lunch *dolce*. *Torta della Nonna*, literally translated as 'grandmother's cake', as an ode to its humble and comforting flavours and textures, is composed of a lemon-scented custard baked inside a double pastry crust (top and bottom – which I suppose technically classifies it as a pie) and topped with pine nuts. The pastry lid makes it unusual, as most custard tart manifestations are topless, but something about the textural difference between two layers of crisp buttery crust sandwiching a wobbling lemony custard is doubly delightful.

I have made the custard quantity slightly larger than in some recipes, because if there is one thing I can't abide it's meanness with custard. For this reason, I use a slightly higher-sided tart tin, though you can make it in a regular flan dish.

Serves 12

For the pastry

300 g (10½ oz/2½ cups) 00 or plain (all-purpose) flour
100 g (3½ oz/¾ cups) icing (confectioner's) sugar
pinch of salt
200 g (7 oz) butter
1 whole egg and 1 egg yolk
1 tsp vanilla extract
zest of 1 lemon, plus 1 tsp of the juice

For the custard filling

750 ml (25 fl oz/3 cups) whole milk
4 strips of lemon zest
120 g (4 oz) egg yolk (5–6 medium yolks)
120 g (4 oz/½ cup) sugar
60 g (2 oz/½ cup) cornflour (cornstarch)

For the pastry, put the flour, icing sugar, salt and butter in the bowl of a stand mixer and pulse until you have fine breadcrumbs. Add the egg and yolk along with the vanilla and lemon zest and briefly blend until it comes together as a dough. Remove from the mixer and shape into two equal rounds. Wrap each in clingfilm (plastic wrap) and chill in the fridge.

For the custard filling, gently heat the milk and lemon zest in a saucepan and bring to just below boiling point.

Meanwhile, whisk the yolks with the sugar in a separate heatproof bowl until pale and mousse-like (you can do this by hand – no need to use a mixer, just a good whisking). Whisk in the cornflour and set aside.

Once the milk is just beginning to simmer (little bubbles should appear around the edge), pour it gently in a steady stream over the egg mixture, whisking all the time.

Return the mixture to the pan and cook over a gentle heat, whisking constantly, until you have a thick custard that coats the back of a wooden spoon. You're aiming for the same consistency as a thick mayonnaise, and it will firm up further once chilled.

Remove the pan from the heat and pour the custard quickly into a container to cool. Remove the strips of lemon with tongs (or your fingers – without burning them!) and discard them. Cover the surface of the custard with clingfilm, to prevent it from forming a skin, and leave it to cool completely.

To finish

1 egg, beaten, or a little milk, to brush the top
20 g (¾ oz) pine nuts
icing (confectioner's) sugar, to dust

Preheat the oven to 170°C (340°F/Gas 3). Grease a 23 cm (9 in) x 5 cm (2 in) deep tart tin or pie dish (see introduction). Roll out one round of the (rested) pastry to 2–3 mm thickness and line the pie dish with it.

Place in the fridge to cool and firm up for at least 20 minutes. Line with baking parchment and blind-bake for 13–15 minutes, until golden and biscuity. (See p 236 for more about blind-baking.) Remove and allow to cool.

Spread the cooled custard over the cold pastry base. If your custard is very lumpy and has developed a skin, whisk it to smooth it out before spreading it in the pie. Roll out the other round of pastry and place over the top, trimming and sealing the edges well by pressing down with your fingers.

Prick the surface several times with a fork. Brush the top with the beaten egg or milk and bake in the oven for around 30 minutes. Open the oven and scatter over the pine nuts (this is to ensure they cook to golden but not brown). Close the oven and continue to cook for a further 20–25 minutes, until both pastry and pine nuts are golden brown.

Remove from the oven and allow to cool completely (this tart is best when eaten on the colder side of room temperature). Dust with icing sugar and serve.

3

CAKES

Torte

Rather confusingly known as *torte,* cakes hold an important place in Italian hearts, as they do in English ones. The two staple cakes of Italian home baking are the Yoghurt Pot Cake (which I included in my book *Bitter Honey*) and *Torta di Mele* (see p 107). Both are especially suited to breakfast, as they are simple, homely and incredibly easy to make.

There are cakes that are everyday cakes, and then there are cakes that are occasion cakes, or fancy cakes, suitable for celebrations, high days and holidays – such as *Cassata* on page 88 and Roasted Nut, Amaretto, Vanilla Bean & Dark Chocolate Cake on page 108. There are also cakes that are suitable as pudding cakes, which are especially decadent and rich, and possibly a little more work to achieve, such as the Chocolate, Pear, Hazelnut & Brown Sugar Cake on page 94 and the Citrus, Campari & Yoghurt Upside-Down Cake on page 84. In short, there is a cake for every occasion.

When considering cakes – something I do surprisingly often – there are three essential factors to take into account: flavour, effort and texture. I want all of my cakes to be moist with a tender crumb, preferably damp enough to keep for at least four days or so.

In terms of effort, a large proportion of the recipes require only a few stages, and a pleasing number of them are made by simply putting everything at once into a blender, which is extremely satisfying.

Caramelised Apricot, Almond & Orange Blossom Upside-Down Cake

This cake is one of the best cakes I have ever made. It's a little chewy at the edges, tart and juicy on the top, moist, squidgy and buttery inside. The tartness of the apricots marries perfectly with the almonds and cuts through the richness of the sponge; the caramelised top adds an edge of fudgy-intrigue, and the exotic scent of orange blossom lifts the whole lot into the arena of the angels.

Upside-down cakes are great for many reasons (see p 259). Laying the fruit at the bottom of the tin takes far less time than decorating the top of a cake/tart with fruit, for some inexplicable reason, and looks just as (if not more) effective. In this arrangement, you have essentially captured both the shining, caramel-glory of a *Tarte Tatin* and the tart dampness of a good fruit sponge. It is the best of both worlds, almost like having your cake and eating it.

Serves 8–10

For the apricots

15 g (½ oz) butter, plus extra for greasing
7–8 apricots
140 g (4½ oz/⅔ cup) sugar
60 ml (4 tbsp) water
1 tbsp lemon juice (use the same lemon for the zest)

For the cake

175 g (6 oz) butter, softened, plus extra to grease
175 g (6 oz) caster (superfine) sugar
a pinch of sea salt
zest of 1 lemon
3 eggs
100 g (3½ oz/¾ cups, plus 2 tbsp) 00 or plain (all-purpose) flour
100 g (3½ oz/1 cup) ground almonds (almond meal)
100 ml (3½ fl oz/scant ½ cup) yoghurt, plus extra to serve
2 tsp baking powder
1 tbsp orange blossom water
mascarpone, to serve (optional)

Grease a 23cm (9 in) cake tin with butter and line with baking parchment. Preheat the oven to 180°C (350°F/Gas 4).

Halve the apricots and remove the stones. Set aside.

Put the sugar and water in a saucepan and heat gently, swirling the pan rather than stirring to dissolve the sugar. Watch carefully until the mixture turns a light coffee colour, swirling occasionally to make sure the caramelisation is even. When the mixture is caramel-coloured, remove from the heat.

Add the butter and turn the heat down to low, stirring until it all comes together. Add the lemon juice and stir well. You should now have a smooth caramel.

Pour the liquid caramel into the lined cake tin and smooth it out to form an even layer. Add the apricots, placing them close to each other, cut-side down.

For the cake, in a mixing bowl and using an electric mixer (or in the bowl of a stand mixer), cream the butter and sugar with the salt and lemon zest until pale and fluffy. Beat in the eggs, one by one, until incorporated. Add the flour and the ground almonds and mix again. Finally add the yoghurt, baking powder and the orange blossom water. Stir to form a smooth batter, then ladle into the prepared tin.

Smooth the top, then bake in the oven for 45–50 minutes, until golden and risen. Allow to cool for a few minutes before inverting onto a serving plate. Serve with yoghurt or a blob of mascarpone.

Note

If you can't find apricots or they aren't in season, you can use tinned ones, which work surprisingly well.

Citrus, Campari & Yoghurt Upside-Down Cake

Another grown-up cake, this one, but a very great one. Citrussy, light, moist, and with the slightly bitter kick of Campari in the background of every bite. The texture is perfectly damp and melt-in-the-mouth. If you can make this with blood oranges when they're in season, it's even more impressive to look at.

This is a cake that could also work as a pudding. It's fancy enough in terms of aesthetics, and sophisticated enough in terms of flavour. Serve it in slices with some extra yoghurt on the side.

If you wish to omit the upside-down decoration feel free to do so; this is still a very good simple cake, even unadorned. (See p 259 for more on upside-down cakes.)

Serves 10–12

For the upside-down decoration

- 40 ml (3 tbsp) Campari
- 2 tbsp water
- 3 tbsp sugar
- 2 oranges, finely sliced

For the cake

- 80 g (3 oz) butter, melted, plus extra for greasing
- 160 ml (5½ fl oz/⅔ cup) yoghurt, plus extra to serve (optional)
- 120 ml (4 fl oz/½ cup) mild light olive oil
- 3 eggs, lightly beaten
- 80 ml (2½ fl oz/5 tbsp) Campari
- zest and juice of 2 small oranges and 1 small lemon (around 100 ml/3½ fl oz/scant ½ cup of juice)
- 300 g (10½ oz/1⅓ cups) sugar
- 225 g (8 oz/1¾ cups, plus 2 tbsp) 00 or plain (all-purpose) flour
- 1 tbsp baking powder
- good pinch salt

Preheat the oven to 180°C (350°F/Gas 4). Grease a 23 cm (9 in) cake tin with butter and line with baking parchment.

To make the decoration, put the Campari, water and sugar in a large saucepan and bring to a simmer. Leave to simmer and reduce for 2 minutes. Lay the orange slices gently in the syrup, spreading them over the base in a single layer so they cook evenly and cover with a cartouche (see p 255). Simmer on a low heat (making sure the sugar doesn't catch at the edges of the pan) for 8–10 minutes until the oranges are just tender and pink all the way through. Remove from the heat and allow to cool a little.

Arrange the orange slices in the base of the prepared tin and gently pour over the syrup from the pan. Set aside.

For the cake, whisk the butter, yoghurt, olive oil, eggs, Campari and the zest and juice of the oranges and lemon in a mixing bowl. Add the sugar and mix until smooth.

Whisk in the flour, baking powder and salt, and mix until you have a smooth batter (it will be quite runny).

Pour the batter into the prepared tin very gently, making sure not to dislodge your arranged orange slices.

Bake for 50 minutes to 1 hour, using a skewer or spaghetti strand to check it's done (see p 252). Allow to cool completely.

Carefully invert onto a plate and serve with extra yoghurt, if you like.

Candied Clementine, Fennel Seed & Polenta Cake

I dreamt up this cake when I was eating an orange and fennel salad. I thought to myself, this combination is so good, and fennel is so sweet and fragrant, that it tastes almost like pudding. Perhaps it could be?

Fennel seeds add a faintly anise back-note, and are often used in Italian cakes and biscuits. They match beautifully with citrus. The polenta gives the cake a pleasing grittiness. Try to find really good, juicy clementines.

This also works very well as a loaf cake, if you'd prefer to make it that way.

Serves 8–10

For the candied clementines

4 clementines
350g (12 oz/1⅔ cups) sugar

For the cake

250 g (9 oz) unsalted butter at room temperature, plus extra for greasing
250 g (9 oz/1 cup, plus 2 tbsp) sugar
pinch of salt
4 eggs
190 g (6½ oz/1½ cups) 00 or plain (all-purpose) flour
150 g (5 oz/1 cup) polenta or fine cornmeal
2 tsp fennel seeds, gently ground in a pestle and mortar, plus extra to garnish
1 tbsp baking powder
zest and juice of 5 tart clementines
3 tbsp natural yoghurt, plus extra to serve

To candy the clementines, follow the method for Cheat's Candied Clementines (see p 231) .

Preheat the oven to 160°C/320°F/Gas 2. Grease a 23 cm (9 in) cake tin with butter and line with baking parchment.

For the cake, in a mixing bowl using an electric whisk (or in the bowl of a stand mixer), beat the butter, sugar and salt until light and fluffy. Add the eggs, one by one, mixing well between additions, until incorporated. Fold in the flour, polenta, fennel seeds and baking powder. Mix the zest and juice of the clementines with the yoghurt and stir this into the mixture.

Spoon the mixture into the prepared tin and bake for around 50 minutes. Insert a skewer or spaghetti strand to check it's done (see p 252).

Leave to cool on a wire rack, then transfer to a serving plate and garnish with the candied clementines and their syrup.

Sprinkle with a few extra fennel seeds, if you like, and serve with a large dollop of yoghurt.

Cassata

If it ain't baroque, don't fix it.

The triumph, the glistening jewel, the crowning glory of baroque extravagance and rococo decoration, the Queen of the Italian pastry canon, has to be *Cassata*.

This extraordinarily lavish cake is composed of layers of simple sponge (*Pan di Spagna*) layered with a sweetened ricotta cream flecked with dark chocolate chips, wrapped in vivid green marzipan and topped with swirls, flowers and strips of candied fruit, most commonly with *zuccata*, or candied pumpkin. Though, like most traditionally festive *dolci*, *Cassate* are now eaten perennially all over Italy, they were originally prepared specifically for Easter. They have become a standard for numerous non-Paschal celebrations: birthdays, christenings, Christmas – any excuse for this gloriously flamboyant concoction, which is truly a coloured and curlicued celebration of sugar and its decorative and delicious qualities.

Before the Arabs introduced sugar cane cultivation to Sicily, from whence it spread to the rest of Italy, the only sweeteners used in Italian *dolci* were honey and *vincotto* (*sapa* or grape must). These tended to imbue everything with a similar (and pronounced) flavour. The cultivation and widespread use of sugar (and its mercurial qualities when used in patisserie) allowed for elaborate, decorative and highly flavoured desserts such as *Cassata* to be born. While historians quibble over whether it derives its name from the Arabic word for the terracotta dish in which it was originally made (*qas'at*) or from the Latin for cheese (*caseus*), it owes its composition to both civilisations, another *dolce* that represents the layers of Sicilian history: Spanish sponge, Roman ricotta, Arabic sugar decoration and *canditi* (candied fruit).

There are as many variations of *Cassata* as there are cooks. Some choose to soak the sponge, others not; some add chocolate, some don't; some taint the marzipan green with pistachio paste. This is the way I make it, based on a combination of recipes I have read about and tried.

This is a project, a special occasion type thing that you will want to spread over a day or two. The ricotta needs to drain for at least a few hours, preferably overnight. Once the ricotta is drained and the sponge and marzipan are made the rest is really very quick and easy.

You will need a 23–24 cm (9–9½ in) cake or pie tin about 10 cm (4 in) deep – ideally with sloping sides. If you can't find one like this, you can use a regular straight-sided tin; the *Cassata* will just have a slightly different look.

Note

The *ghiaccia reale* gives the white swirls if you wish to add these. It is a little extra effort, but looks wonderfully decorative and lace-like. You can also buy ready-made royal icing if you prefer, but it needs to be pipe-able. You can also freeze the marzipan.

continued →

Il Bricolage del Dolce
Pasticceria
Decorazioni
Oristano
Via Arborea, 30
Cell. 339 8636289

continued →

Serves 10–12

1 x *Pan di Spagna* (see Fatless Sponge, p 238)

For the marzipan
(You can buy 250 g/9 oz of ready-made marzipan if you prefer)

150 g (5 oz) blanched almonds, ground to a fine powder in a food processor (or use 150 g/5 oz/1½ cups ready-ground almonds)
150 g (5 oz/1¼ cups) icing (confectioner's) sugar, plus extra to dust
1 tablespoon lemon juice
1 tablespoon water
a few drops of green food colouring

Make the sponge according to the instructions on page 238.

Line the cake tin with cling film (plastic wrap), covering it evenly and smoothly, leaving plenty of extra hanging over the sides.

Make the marzipan. Put the ground almonds in a bowl, add the icing sugar, lemon juice and water, and knead together for a few minutes until you have a smooth dough (it will be a little sticky but will dry out as you work it). Knead in the green dye. Wrap in cling film and set aside. (If using ready-made, just dye it green by kneading in the food colouring.)

Make the syrup by bringing the Marsala, sugar and orange zest to a simmer in a small saucepan. Simmer until the sugar has melted, then set aside and stir in the orange blossom water.

Cut the sponge lengthways into thin slices (roughly 1 cm/½ in thick) using a sharp serrated knife.

For the filling push the drained ricotta through the sieve in which it has been draining using a spoon (this helps create a smooth uniform consistency). Add the sugar and beat thoroughly until smooth and creamy. Fold through the chocolate chips/shards and set aside.

For the soaking syrup

50 ml (4 tbsp) Marsala
30 g (1 oz/2½ tbsp) sugar
4 strips of orange zest
1 tbsp orange blossom water

For the filling

800 g (1 lb 12 oz) ricotta (preferably fresh sheep's milk ricotta, rather than supermarket stuff), thoroughly drained in a sieve for a few hours, or overnight
200 g (7 oz/¾ cup plus 2 tbsp) sugar
50 g (2 oz) dark chocolate chips or shards

For the icing

180 g (6¼ oz/1½ cups) icing (confectioner's) sugar
30 ml (2 tbsp) lemon juice
candied fruit, to decorate

For the *ghiaccia reale* (royal icing)

150g (5 oz/1¼ cup) icing (confectioner's) sugar
1 egg white

Roll out the marzipan with your hands into a long sausage shape, then roll the sausage with a rolling pin into a long oval 5 mm (¼ in) thick, dusting the work surface with icing sugar. Cut two long strips about 7.5 cm (3 in) in width. Line the sides of the tin with these strips, trimming where necessary and patching up any seams or overlaps by pressing with your fingertips.

Lay the strips of sponge to cover the base of the tin and create a smooth layer, pressing down gently. Reserve enough to cover the top.

Paint the sponge with a pastry brush dipped in the syrup, not soaking but dabbing daintily.

Spoon over the ricotta mixture and spread in an even layer. Top with the remaining sponge to form a smooth layer and trim any overhang. Paint the sponge again with the syrup.

Cover the whole thing with the overhanging bits of cling film and weigh down with a plate. Leave in the fridge to chill for at least 1 hour or overnight.

Remove from the fridge and invert onto a plate or cake board.

Make the icing by mixing the icing sugar with the lemon juice, using just enough so that it is just at pouring consistency. Press down the sponge top of the *Cassata*, creating space for the icing to fill (the lip of marzipan will contain it nicely), then pour the icing gently over the sponge to create an even white layer. Leave to set for 1 hour. Decorate with candied fruit.

If making the *ghiaccia reale*, whisk the icing sugar with the egg white in a mixing bowl using an electric whisk (or in the bowl of a stand mixer fitted with the beater attachment). Whisk well for a few minutes until the icing is opaque and white, like meringue. Make a tiny piping bag with a piece of greaseproof paper (or use a disposable piping bag, just cutting the tiniest tip off to create a very small hole) and transfer some of the icing into it. Cut the tip off to create a tiny nozzle and then gently pipe patterns onto the *Cassata*. Allow the icing to set hard before serving.

Note

Cassata is traditionally made with slightly sloping sides 7.5–10 cm (3–4 in) deep. I have a specially made tin for this purpose, and you can order them online, but you can also forgo the sloping sides and make it in a spring-form cake tin if you prefer.

Almond, Ricotta, Olive Oil & Cherry Cake

Another cake that demands little in terms of preparation, but that delivers in aesthetics and flavour. Cherries and ricotta are a classic combination, as are cherries and almonds, and both with good reason.

Serves 8–10

melted butter, for greasing
280 g (10 oz) cherries, stoned
zest and juice of 1 large lemon
250 g (9 oz) ricotta
200 ml (7 fl oz/scant 1 cup) olive oil
4 eggs
100 g (3½ oz/1 cup) ground almonds (almond meal)
150 g (5 oz/1¼ cups) 00 or plain (all-purpose) flour
2 tsp baking powder
200 g (7 oz/¾ cup, plus 2 tbsp) sugar
good pinch of salt
40 g (1½ oz) flaked almonds
icing (confectioner's) sugar, to dust

Preheat the oven to 180°C (350°F/Gas 4).

Using a pastry brush, grease a 23 cm (9 in) cake tin with melted butter and line with baking parchment.

Toss the cherries in a bowl with the lemon juice and zest then set aside to macerate for 1–2 minutes.

Put all of the remaining ingredients, except for the flaked almonds and icing sugar, in a blender and blend to a smooth batter. (If you do not have a blender you can whisk everything together by hand in a mixing bowl using a balloon whisk, starting with the ricotta and oil to make sure there are no lumps in the ricotta, then adding the eggs and whisking, then finally whisking in the dry ingredients.) Stir through half of the cherries.

Pour the batter into the prepared tin and spread it out evenly. Sprinkle over the remaining cherries and the flaked almonds.

Bake the cake until risen and golden, 40–45 minutes. Insert a skewer or spaghetti strand to check it's done (see p 252).

Set aside to cool for 10 minutes before turning out onto a wire rack to cool completely. Transfer to a serving plate, dust with icing sugar and serve.

Note

You can use frozen cherries if you wish; they work surprisingly well.

Chocolate, Pear, Hazelnut & Brown Sugar Cake

The combination of pears and chocolate is a nostalgic one for me, as one of my mum's signature puddings when I was growing up was a soft, liquid-centred chocolate cake with tinned pears set inside it. It's a happy marriage, and one I am only too happy to re-interpret and recreate in Italy.

I feel that everybody should have one flourless chocolate cake recipe up their sleeve; the Little Black Dress of the cake world. Based (very loosely) on a *Torta Caprese*, a classic chocolate cake from Capri, this is the one I have, which has a lovely depth thanks to the brown sugar, and feels a little autumnal, thanks to the pears and hazelnuts. As this is essentially a baked chocolate mousse, the texture inside is moist and fudgy, and it is much lighter in the eating than it perhaps looks.

You can add the pear pieces raw if you are short on time, but they are nicer (and more reminiscent of the tinned pears my mum used) when poached first, as they become more giving in texture and their flavour is intensified.

Serves 8–10

For the pears

3 tbsp sugar
300 ml (10 fl oz/1¼ cups) water
2 medium pears, peeled, cored and sliced into eighths

For the cake

melted butter, for greasing
100 g (3½ oz) hazelnuts
150 g (5 oz) dark chocolate
150 g (5 oz) butter, cut into pieces
pinch of salt
4 eggs, separated
130 g (4 oz) brown sugar (Demerara or light muscovado)
mascarpone or pouring cream, to serve

For the pears, bring the sugar and water to a simmer in a saucepan. Add the pear pieces, cover with a cartouche (see p 255) and poach over a low heat for 10 minutes or until tender. Drain the pear pieces (you can use the poaching liquid in another recipe) and allow the pears to cool.

Preheat the oven to 170°C (340°F/Gas 3). Using a pastry brush, grease a 22–23 cm (8–9 in) cake tin with melted butter and line with baking parchment. (This cake rises then sinks a lot once cooked, so I make it in a smaller 22 cm/8½ in tin to give it some extra height, but you can use a 23 cm/9 in tin if that's all you have).

Spread the hazelnuts over the base of a baking sheet and roast in the oven until golden. In a blender or food processor (or in a pestle and mortar), grind the hazelnuts to a fine rubble.

Melt the chocolate, butter and salt in a heatproof bowl set over a pan of barely simmering water (don't let the base of the bowl touch the water). Once completely melted, set aside to cool for 1–2 minutes.

Stir the egg yolks gently into the cooled chocolate mixture until incorporated.

In a clean, grease-free mixing bowl, whisk the egg whites with the brown sugar to form soft, shiny peaks (they will look creamy when they are ready, and be akin to softly whipped cream).

Stir the ground hazelnuts gently into the chocolate mixture, then fold in the egg whites. (See notes on folding, p 256.)

Spoon the mixture into the prepared tin and top with the poached pear slices. Bake for 30–35 minutes, until just set in the middle.

Allow to cool for 10 minutes before turning out and serving with a dollop of mascarpone or some pouring cream.

Almond, Ricotta, Olive Oil & Lemon Drizzle Cake

This is another creation based around one of my favourite English cake classics, the saintly lemon drizzle. Like the great lemon drizzle, this cake is moist, citrussy and extremely satisfying to make and eat. Unlike a traditional lemon drizzle, there is no whipping or creaming of butter involved.

This cake is infinitely adaptable, a perfect building block to which you can add as you see fit, to suit any and every occasion that life might throw at you. If you wish to omit the drizzle, the cake makes a very good, solid, simple sort of breakfast cake, a little more humbly cakey in texture, but very good with a coffee. If you like the citrus-soaked, moist glory of the lemon drizzle, then add the syrup. You can then choose to ice it with a simple glaze icing for an extra flourish.

Serves 8–10

For the cake

melted butter, for greasing
250 g (9 oz) ricotta
200 ml (7 fl oz/scant 1 cup) olive oil
100 g (3½ oz/1 cup) ground almonds
150 g (5 oz/1¼ cups) 00 or plain (all-purpose) flour
2 tsp baking powder
200g (7 oz/¾ cup, plus 2 tbsp) sugar
good pinch of salt
4 eggs
zest of 3 lemons (small) or 2 large (reserve the juice for the syrup, below)

For the syrup

70 g (2½ oz/⅓ cup) sugar
juice of 3 small lemons (or 2 large)

For the glaze (optional)

1 x Lemon Glaze Icing (see p 238)

Preheat the oven to 180°C (350°F/Gas 4).

Using a pastry brush, grease a 23 cm (9 in) cake tin with melted butter (you can use a bundt or a standard round tin).

Put all the remaining cake ingredients in a blender and blend to a smooth batter. (If you do not have a blender you can whisk everything together by hand in a mixing bowl using a balloon whisk, starting with the ricotta and then the oil to make sure there are no lumps in the ricotta.)

Pour the batter into the prepared tin and spread it out evenly.

Bake until risen and golden, 40–45 minutes. Insert a skewer or spaghetti strand to check it's done (see p 252).

Allow the cake to cool while you make the syrup. Melt the sugar and lemon juice in a small saucepan and simmer for a few minutes until syrupy. Pour the syrup over the cake and leave to cool completely before turning it out onto a serving plate (you can poke holes in the cake before pouring over the syrup to make absorption faster).

Make the glaze (if using) following the instructions on page 238. Drizzle the glaze over the cake before serving.

Ricotta, Pear & Hazelnut Layer Cake

This classic southern Italian cake originated in the late 1990s in Minori, created by the renowned pastry chef, Sal de Riso for his eponymous pastry shop. It has subsequently made its way around various parts of Italy and acquired a well-deserved hallowed status in the *dolci* hall of fame. Little surprise, as it is a beauty to look at and to eat, and is impossibly chic without requiring too much effort. As with the *Sbriciolata* recipe (see p 66), there is something about a thick layer of white and creamy filling sandwiched between two camel-brown crusts that is instantly celebratory and appealing.

The hazelnut cake is light and nutty, gently soaked in the pear-poaching liquor, and the creamy ricotta filling complements it perfectly. A wonderfully light and elegant thing, perfect to take as a pudding as it can be made the night before and benefits from a night sitting in the fridge to firm up.

Serves 8–10

For the cake

170 g (6 oz) hazelnuts
100 g (3½ oz) butter, plus extra for greasing
3 eggs
150 g (5 oz/⅔ cup) sugar
70 g (2½ oz/½ cup, plus 2 tbsp) 00 or plain (all-purpose) flour
pinch of salt

For the ricotta filling

600 g (1 lb 5 oz) ricotta
150 g (5 oz/⅔ cup) sugar
300 ml (10 fl oz/1¼ cups) cream

For the pears

300 g (10½ oz) pears (4–5 small pears)
50 g (2 oz/¼ cup) sugar
zest and juice of 1 lemon
100 ml (3½ fl oz/scant ½ cup) water
half a vanilla pod (bean) or a few drops of extract

Preheat the oven to 170°C (340°F/Gas 3). Spread the hazelnuts over the base of a baking sheet and toast in the oven for 10 minutes or so, until light brown. Remove and set aside to cool. Turn the oven temperature up to 180°C (350°F/Gas 4).

Now make the cake. You will make one cake, which will be cut in half to form two layers. Grease a 23 cm (9 in) spring-form cake tin with butter and line with baking parchment.

Beat the eggs with the sugar in the bowl of a stand mixer or in a mixing bowl using an electric mixer until pale, fluffy and mousse-like. This will take a good few minutes, and they should triple in volume.

Melt the butter (in a small saucepan or in the microwave) and set aside to cool.

Grind the hazelnuts to a fine powder in a food processor and fold them through the egg mixture, along with the flour and salt. Fold in the melted butter and pour the batter into the prepared tin.

Bake in the oven for 20–30 minutes, until risen, set and golden. Insert a skewer or spaghetti strand to check it's done (see p 252). Remove from the oven and set aside to cool.

Once cool, remove from the tin and slice carefully in half horizontally (I use a strong piece of thread to do this, pulling it through the cake to slice it cleanly in half).

For the filling, beat the ricotta and sugar in a mixing bowl until completely smooth (this will take a good few minutes, especially if you have good ricotta which is denser).

In a separate bowl whip the cream to firm peaks. Fold the cream through the ricotta mixture.

continued →

continued →

Peel and core the pears. Cut them into 2.5 cm (1 in) pieces and place them in a small saucepan with the sugar, lemon zest, water and vanilla pod or extract. Bring to a gentle simmer and poach the pieces very gently for 10 minutes, or until they are tender and translucent. Remove from the heat and stir in the lemon juice. Strain through a sieve, catching all the syrup in a bowl to use later. Remove the zest and vanilla pod and discard.

Paint the exposed sponge layers with the syrup using a pastry brush. Place the bottom half of the cake on the base of the springform cake tin with the ring around it, to help you build your cake and keep the sides contained.

Stir the strained, cooled pear pieces into the ricotta mixture, then spread the mixture on top of the sponge in the tin. Place the other sponge half on top (fitting it into the cake tin) and press down gently.

Transfer the cake to the fridge and leave to set for at least a few hours, ideally overnight.

Release the cake from the tin and transfer to a serving plate. Sprinkle with icing sugar before serving.

Note

This is one of those occasions where you will really need to buy good quality ricotta. The supermarket stuff tends to be too wet and grainy. See notes on ricotta on page 76.

You can decorate the cake with some extra hazelnuts and/or a slice of candied pear.

Spiced Pumpkin Cake with Orange & Mascarpone Icing

I love pumpkin in sweet and savoury recipes, and I was delighted to discover that it is often baked into cakes in Italy. The grated flesh gives an earthy depth, sweetness and moistness to the cake as well as being undeniably autumnal. This *Torta di Zucca* is the *cavallo di battaglia* (battle horse, or secret weapon) of one of my friend's aunts, who serves it unfrosted, though I love this rich, creamy icing so much I am loathe to part with it, however good the cake may be on its own.

You can use any sweet eating pumpkin or squash for this, such as butternut, crown prince or onion squash.

Serves 8–10

120 g (4 oz) butter, at room temperature, plus extra for greasing
200 g (7 oz) pumpkin, peeled and finely grated
zest and juice of 1 orange
70 ml (2½ fl oz/5 tbsp) light olive or seed oil
230 g (8 oz) light brown sugar
3 eggs
½ tsp salt
½ tsp ground cinnamon
250 g (9 oz/2 cups) 00 or plain (all-purpose) flour
1 tbsp baking powder

For the icing

zest of 1 orange plus 1 tbsp juice
250 g (9 oz) mascarpone
180 g (6¼ oz) full-fat Philadelphia cream cheese
100 g (3½ oz/¾ cup) icing (confectioner's) sugar

To decorate

orange zest, sprinkles or candied orange slices

Preheat the oven to 180°C (350°F/Gas 4).

Butter 2 × 22 cm (8½ in) sandwich tins and line the bases with baking parchment. Put the grated pumpkin in a bowl and add the orange zest and juice.

In a large mixing bowl and using an electric mixer (or in the bowl of a stand mixer), beat the butter, oil and sugar until pale, smooth and fluffy, with a light *caffe latté* colour. Add the eggs one at a time, beating well after each addition, until they are fully incorporated.

Add the salt, cinnamon, flour, baking powder and, finally, the grated pumpkin and orange mix, and stir to combine.

Spoon the batter into the prepared tins, dividing it equally and smoothing the tops. Bake in the oven for 25–30 minutes, until risen and golden. Insert a skewer or spaghetti strand to check it's done (see p 252).

Remove from the oven and allow to cool for 10 minutes before turning out of the tins and leaving to cool completely on a wire rack.

Beat the ingredients for the icing together in a mixing bowl. Spread half of the icing over the base of the cake, sandwiching it with the top half, then spread the remainder of the icing on top.

Decorate with orange zest or sprinkles, as you see fit. Some slivers of candied orange would also be nice.

Cream, Custard and Lactic Lustre

Cream

Cream in England is a wonderful, varied and lavish thing that I took for granted until I moved away and no longer had access to it. Cream is (unfortunately) not a big part of the Sardinian diet, and in many parts of Italy too it is difficult to find good cream, however hard you look. The cream I have found in my day-to-day shopping tends to be a fairly sorry affair; it pours in a thin dribble and whips to light, empty peaks that are more sweet air than lactic luxury.

In northern parts of Italy, where dairy farming and green pastures are more common, it is perhaps easier to find creams like those I remember from England. Ivory cream, thick enough to stand a spoon up in, seems but a distant memory now, and a wide variety of creams (double, single, pouring, clotted, spooning, thick, Jersey, extra-thick) a long-lost luxury. However, the lack of lactic loveliness in terms of cream is more than made up for with mascarpone.

Mascarpone

Every cloud has a silver lining. When one door closes, another opens, and while good cream may elude me, at least I have mascarpone as a consolation prize.

Mascarpone is one of the joys of the Italian grocery list. Made by adding an acidic coagulant (such as lemon juice) to double cream, it originated in Lombardia, and the true artisanal product (which I have yet to taste) is still aged in wooden containers and purportedly has a fresher flavour than the UHT supermarket stuff.

Nevertheless, the supermarket tubs hold a squat, round place in my heart. Although it could technically be described as cream cheese, that seems almost an injustice, because to me mascarpone is more lovely in texture and flavour than a standard cream cheese. The flavour is slightly less tangy, and the texture more velvety and luscious.

This is because mascarpone has a higher fat content (around 75 per cent compared to cream cheese's 55 per cent). It also has an irresistible texture somewhere between butter and thick cream; the sort of texture that dents and forms snowy contours and peaks when a spoon is dragged through it, the sort of texture that is infinitely satisfying to scoop (and irresistible not to prod a fingertip into).

Mascarpone can be eaten alongside cakes instead of whipped cream or crème fraîche, and makes a wonderful filling for cheesecakes. When perfumed with citrus or vanilla and sweetened with icing (confectioner's) sugar it is the perfect thick and luxurious filling for tarts or icing for cakes. It is endlessly versatile and inexpensive, and I always have a back-up tub or two in the fridge (it is also good in savoury recipes).

Making mascarpone

You can easily make mascarpone at home, should you wish to, or if it proves hard to find. It's a nice soothing thing to do, as it is so straightforward and children will enjoy the alchemic process.

You will need 2 teaspoons of lemon juice for every half-litre (17 fl oz) of cream.

Put the cream in a heavy-based saucepan over a medium heat and bring it to a scald (just below boiling – you will see small bubbles forming around the edge of the pan), then remove the pan from the heat.

Add the lemon juice and stir gently. Line a sieve with a piece of cheesecloth or muslin, set it over a bowl and pour the cream into it. Leave the whole lot overnight (or for a few hours at least) in the fridge and – *voila*! Your very own artisanal mascarpone made from just two easy, everyday ingredients.

Custard dreams

Custard is semi-solid, eggy evidence of the existence of divinity. The wobble, bounce, ooze and squirt of it, the round and curved and voluptuous shapes and contours and swathes and folds and blobs and explosions of it. I don't think there is any happier sight than custard bursting forth from an amply filled bun or doughnut, or any happier feeling than biting into said bun/doughnut and feeling your teeth break through soft, bouncy dough into softer, silkier custard. Cheerily yellow, blobbily bright and seductively shiny, custard is happiness in edible form.

Custard, technically, is a preparation of cream or milk cooked with eggs and occasionally cornflour (cornstarch), or flour to thicken it. Some claim true custard should have no flour-based thickener, and should instead rely on eggs to thicken it, but I like the extra bounce and body a little cornflour gives, so I add it in various quantities to all of my custard recipes. Bird's custard, the cheerful coloured packet so familiar to many Brits, is not technically custard at all, containing all cornflour and no eggs as it does. I have a sentimental fondness for it, however, as I do for Ambrosia, which was a treat when I was a child, and one reason we bristled with pride to be born in Devon.

Just contemplating custard makes me feel better, and as far as I am concerned there is no bad version. The custard for the decadent Quince, Bay, Marsala & Hazelnut Trifle on page 132 is made with a large quantity of cream, which makes it extra-rich, while the others (such as the one for the *Bomboloni* (see p 152) and the *Torta della Nonna* (see p 78) are made with milk, making them slightly lighter. My choice to add cornflour not only adds to the bounce and wobble of the custard but also means it is easier to cook and less likely to curdle.

The One True Apple Cake

There is a cake that almost every mother and grandmother in Italy makes (the sister of the Yoghurt Pot Cake which featured in *Bitter Honey*) and is one of the simplest cakes of all, and that cake is *Torta di Mele*. It is to the Italians what Victoria sponge is to the English: the epitome of comforting, nostalgic home baking. It is a domestic institution, and is most often eaten for breakfast or *merenda*, with a strong coffee.

Choose whichever apple is your favourite to eat, and keep the skin on; the colours look lovely.

Serves 10–12

- 170 g (6 oz) butter, at room temperature, plus extra, for greasing
- 5 eating (dessert) apples
- zest and juice of 1 lemon
- 220 g (8 oz/1 cup) sugar, plus 2 tbsp for sprinkling
- 1 tsp vanilla extract
- pinch of salt
- 3 eggs
- 100 ml (3½ fl oz/scant ½ cup) yoghurt
- 30 ml (2 tbsp) light olive or seed oil
- 1 tbsp baking powder
- 250 g (9 oz/2 cups) 00 or plain (all-purpose) flour
- icing (confectioner's) sugar, for dusting

Preheat the oven to 180°C (350°F/Gas 4). Grease a 23 cm (9 in) cake tin with butter and line with baking parchment.

Core 3½ of the apples and cut them into small chunks. Slice the remaining apple into crescent-shaped wedges to decorate the top of the cake. Squeeze the lemon juice over the apples to stop them from going brown.

In a mixing bowl, beat the butter with the sugar, lemon zest, vanilla extract and salt until pale and fluffy. Add the eggs one at a time, beating well between additions until smooth. Beat in the yoghurt and the oil, then fold in the baking powder and the flour and finally the chopped apples. Mix together until you have a nice smooth batter.

Pour into the prepared tin, decorate with the apple slices and sprinkle over the extra sugar.

Bake in the oven for 45–50 minutes until risen and golden then insert a skewer or spaghetti strand to check it's done (see p 252). Allow to cool for 10 minutes in the tin before turning out onto a wire rack.

Dust with icing sugar and serve warm or cool.

Roasted Nut, Amaretto, Vanilla Bean & Dark Chocolate Cake

This is the kind of cake you'll want to make for an occasion. Based on a classic River Cafe recipe which I have tinkered with, I made it once for a birthday party, and a friend described it as 'a cake for grown-ups'. I think he meant was that it has such an indulgent flavour and texture that it is definitely not the sort of humble, homely cake you eat every day, more of a showstopper. It's extremely *burrosa,* heady with vanilla, moist with nuts, with a faintly bitter and velvety-smooth chocolate topping, flecked with sea salt. Blitzing (or chopping) the vanilla pods (beans) – skin and all – means you get an intensity of flavour that I have rarely encountered elsewhere.

I love this cake, and it's usually the cake I turn to when I need to make something a bit special, not least because the ingredients are fairly expensive. Good as an alternative Christmas cake too, if you're anti-fruitcake.

Serves 12

250 g (9 oz) almonds
150 g (5 oz) walnuts
2 vanilla pods (beans)
250 g (9 oz) butter, at room temperature, plus extra for greasing
250 g (9 oz/1 cup, plus 2 tbsp) sugar
4 eggs
80 g (3 oz/⅔ cup) 00 or plain (all-purpose) flour
1 tsp baking powder
pinch of salt, plus extra to decorate
100 ml (3½ fl oz/scant ½ cup) Amaretto

For the icing

150 g (5 oz) dark chocolate (at least 70% cocoa solids)
30 g (1 oz) butter

Preheat the oven to 170°C (340°F/Gas 3).

Grease a 23 cm (9 in) cake tin with butter and line with baking parchment.

Spread the almonds and walnuts over the base of a baking tray and roast in the oven for 8–10 minutes, or until golden and beginning to smell good. Blitz them in a food processor (or chop them by hand) until they form a fine rubble (a few pieces slightly bigger than others is nice – though not large chunks. Nothing larger than a peanut.)

Chop the vanilla pods into very small pieces using a sharp knife (using the whole pods means you get a wonderful intensity of flavour). If you have a strong blender you can use that; just make sure you end up with tiny pieces.

Cream the butter and sugar in a mixing bowl using an electric mixer (or in the bowl of a stand mixer) until the mixture is pale and fluffy. Add the vanilla pods and mix to incorporate.

Beat in the eggs, one at a time, little by little, whisking all the time until they are fully incorporated. Mix in the ground nuts, the flour, baking powder, salt and the Amaretto until you have a smooth batter.

Pour the batter into the prepared tin and smooth the top. Bake in the oven for 55 minutes, or until risen, then insert a skewer or spaghetti strand to check it's done (see p 252).

Remove from the oven and allow to cool for 10 minutes in the tin before turning out onto a wire rack to cool completely.

For the icing, melt the chocolate and butter in a bain-marie (see p 255). You could use a microwave if you prefer.

Spread the icing over the top of the cooled cake (I go for a thick top layer but if you want a thinner all-round coverage you can also do the sides).

Allow to cool and sprinkle with the sea salt. Serve, with lots of black coffee.

53

Ditta Leoni
Loc. Pardu Accas pod. 22
Produzione Propria

Yossy's Olive Oil, Rosemary & Yoghurt Cake

Another recipe that is inseparable from a person; the brilliant baker Yossy Arefi made this cake when we worked together at Melisses in Andros, and it fast became a staple back home in Italy. She gave me a wonderful charlotte tin, too, which I always bake it in. I couldn't make it any other way now.

The inclusion of olive oil, rosemary and lemon zest makes it seem easily at home on an Italian breakfast or tea table. It's a light, delicate cake with a tender crumb and a lovely fresh, herby flavour. The perfect thing to serve with some poached fruit and an extra dollop of yoghurt.

Serves 8–10

- 55 g (2 oz) butter, melted, plus extra for greasing
- 225 g (8 oz/1¾ cups, plus 2 tbsp) 00 or plain (all-purpose) flour, plus extra for dusting
- 2 tsp finely chopped fresh rosemary
- grated zest of 1 lemon
- 200 g (7 oz/¾ cup, plus 2 tbsp) sugar
- 175 ml (6 fl oz/¾ cup) olive oil
- 4 large eggs
- 240 ml (8½ fl oz/1 cup) natural yoghurt
- 2 tsp baking powder
- pinch of salt
- icing (confectioner's) sugar, for dusting

Preheat the oven to 180°C (350°F/Gas 4). Using a pastry brush, grease a 23 cm (9 in) cake tin or bundt tin with butter and dust it lightly with flour.

Mix the rosemary, lemon zest and sugar together in a mixing bowl.

Whisk in the olive oil and the melted butter.

Add the eggs and whisk for 30 more seconds.

Whisk in the yoghurt and then fold in the flour, baking powder and salt.

Pour the batter into the prepared tin and level the top.

Bake for 45 minutes, using a skewer or spaghetti strand to check it's done (see p 252). Allow to cool in the tin for 10 minutes before turning out on a wire rack to cool completely.

Dust with icing sugar before serving.

4

SWEETS BY THE SPOON

Dolci al cucchiaio

Sweets by the spoon, or *dolci al cucchiaio*; a lovely phrase for a lovely group of desserts that are soft or melting enough to be scooped up with a spoon. This term generally describes fruit or cream-based desserts, including *Panna Cotta*, *Tiramisù* and *Zuppa Inglese*.

Interestingly, while 'pudding' in England has come to mean all manner of things, *budino*, the Italian word for pudding, is generally employed to describe a very specific type of wobbling confection set with cornflour (cornstarch) and flavoured with chocolate or vanilla (colourful and tempting powdered packets of which I pass frequently in the supermarket). I have yet to try it, though the nostalgic Angel Delight memories it inspires mean that I am resolved to do so.

There are *dolci* to be eaten with fingers and *dolci* to be eaten with forks, gelatos to be licked and biscuits to be dunked, but the following recipes fall into none of these categories, and instead require a dainty teaspoon.

Panna Cotta The Ultimate *Dolce al Cucchiaio*

I've had a weakness for a soft, sweet, seductively set milk jelly ever since I was a child and my grandmother would make us junket.

A little like the junket of my childhood, but somehow more chic and just a touch more solid, is the Italian *Panna Cotta*. Literally translated as 'cooked cream', a *Panna Cotta* is traditionally a cream-based, gelatine-set pudding usually eaten in dainty individual portions with a teaspoon. Many cultures have their own interpretation of a set milk/cream pudding (the English equivalent is the now long-forgotten blancmange) and for good reason too – the cool, creamy, gentle sweetness of such puddings, coupled with their irresistibly sensual texture, is a wobbling and winning way to finish any meal. They provide a perfect balance between richness and delicacy, and are equally good at any time of year.

Panna Cotta is one of the simplest puddings to make, involving no oven and a meagre few minutes of warming and whisking. I think many people fear gelatine, but if you follow the basic recipe on page 118 you cannot fail.

Originally from Piedmont, *Panna Cotta* did not officially appear in Italian recipe books until the 1960s, but it has since become a ubiquitous dessert available in almost every trattoria, alongside the token *Tiramisù*. Here in Sardinia the *Pannas* are invariably the same, often made from a mix (most supermarkets sell a wide range of these ready mixes) and proffered with a choice of two – occasionally three – indisputably bottled syrups: chocolate, fruits of the forest or caramel.

Panna Cottas these days exists in many forms, from those which call for 100 per cent cream to those substituting some of the traditional cream/milk components with varying amounts of buttermilk, sour cream, yoghurt or even labneh. The argument for yoghurt and buttermilk is that their acidity lightens the richness of the *Panna Cotta*, but after extensive experimentation I decided that, for me, this was another of those instances of not changing a winning team. *Panna Cotta* made with yoghurt or buttermilk can be good, but made in this way it stops being *Panna Cotta*, and becomes something else instead.

see recipe on page 118 →

A Perfect *Panna Cotta*

When considering a perfect, pure *Panna Cotta*, there are a few cornerstones:

The flavouring

You can add any flavourings you choose: infuse the cream with toasted nuts (almonds, pistachio), with roasted coffee beans, with strips of citrus zest, with spices (cardamom or saffron are favourites), with herbs (basil is good), with rose water or orange blossom water. Sometimes there is nothing better than real vanilla. The milky, gentle background provides the perfect canvas for its intense aroma and musky sweetness. There is something a little magical about the visual contrast of the tiny black speckles of the vanilla seeds against the milky-white *panna*, like tiny black rabbit tracks in a vast snow-scape.

The set

Almost half of the enjoyment of a *Panna Cotta* is textural. Aim for the soft, gentle wobble of a woman's breast. The perfect *Panna Cotta* should be only just holding its shape. It should shudder as you lift the dish, and quiver with pale-faced expectancy as you lift your spoon and puncture its innocent white purity. You should still feel a little fear when turning it out, which is part of the fun. I'd always rather have one that was too liquid than too solid.

The creaminess

This *Panna Cotta* is unashamedly rich; a celebration of the lovely, lactic sweetness of cream, and thus does not beg the help of yoghurt for lightness or tanginess. For this reason it marries well with tart poached fruit, tart fresh fruit, bitter coffee and toasty nut flavours. The purist's recipe is, of course, very good on its own, but I would like a bitter black espresso afterwards.

Setting and unmoulding

You can set a *Panna Cotta* in whatever vessel you wish, including a bowl, a glass or a ramekin. If you're using dariole moulds and want to serve them unmoulded first lightly oil the moulds with a little flavourless oil using a pastry brush.

To unmould, hold the *Panna* in its mould in a bowl of warm water for a few seconds before inverting it onto the plate (the warm water melts the gelatine slightly and allows the *panna* to slip out).

Perfect Pure *Panna Cotta*

The simplest, purest *Panna Cotta*, flavoured only with vanilla, and with a perfect wobble.

Makes 6 dainty ramekin-size or espresso cup-size *Panna Cottas*

flavourless oil, for oiling the moulds
400 ml (13 fl oz/generous 1½ cups) cream
100 ml (3½ fl oz/scant ½ cup) milk
50 g (2 oz/¼ cup) sugar
1 vanilla pod, split
2 leaves gelatine (3–4 g)

Oil your chosen moulds lightly using a pastry brush. Warm half the cream in a saucepan over a medium heat with the milk, sugar and vanilla pod, then bring to a scald. You will see small bubbles appearing at the edge of the pan when it is ready (see p 259). Remove from the heat.

Slake the gelatine in a bowl of cold water to soften (see p 259).

Squeeze as much moisture as you can from the gelatine, add it to the hot cream mixture and stir well to dissolve. Add the remaining cream to the mixture and strain it through a sieve into a jug, removing the vanilla pod (the vanilla pod can be saved and used in other recipes).

Pour the *Panna Cotta* mixture into the prepared moulds, transfer to the fridge and leave to set for at least 4 hours. Remove from the fridge around 15 minutes before serving to take the chill off.

To serve, turn out the *Panna Cottas* from their moulds onto serving plates.

Roasted Almond *Panna Cotta* with Poached Apricots

Roasting the almonds and then infusing the cream with them yields the most wonderfully toasty, nutty back-note in an otherwise creamily straightforward *Panna Cotta*.

Perhaps you think it is ridiculous to include a recipe for poached fruit, but there is poached fruit and poached fruit in this world, and these are the latter. To make truly great poached fruit, a few simple details should be observed. The first is to make a sugar syrup beforehand, which helps the fruit retain its shape and cooks it thoroughly while imparting sweetness, in a process similar to candying. The second is to flavour the syrup with lemon, which brings out the best in all fruits.

The following recipe is applicable for all stone fruits, and for apples and pears. It is always best eaten cold.

Makes 6 small panna cottas

For the *Panna Cotta*

flavourless oil, for oiling the moulds
200 g (7 oz) whole blanched almonds
2 leaves gelatine (3–4 g)
400 ml (13 fl oz/generous 1½ cups) cream
100 ml (3½ fl oz/scant ½ cup) milk
50 g (2 oz) sugar
2 strips of lemon zest

For the poached apricots

100 ml (3½ fl oz/scant ½ cup) water
160 g (5½ oz) sugar
a few strips of lemon zest
500 g (1 lb 2 oz) apricots, stoned and halved (or other fruit)

Preheat the oven to 170°C (340°F/Gas 3). Oil 6 dariole moulds with flavourless oil using a pastry brush.

Spread the almonds over the base of a baking sheet and roast in the oven until they begin to smell nutty, 8–10 minutes. Remove from the oven and allow to cool a little, then chop them roughly.

Slake the gelatine in a small bowl of cold water until softened (see p 259).

In a small saucepan, warm the cream, milk, sugar and lemon zest, bring the mixture just to a boil, then turn down the heat to low. Stir well to dissolve the sugar, then add the chopped almonds. Remove from the heat. Using your hands, squeeze as much excess water as you can from the softened gelatine, add to the cream mixture and stir well to dissolve.

Using a fine sieve, strain the mixture into a jug (discard the solids), then pour evenly into the prepared dariole moulds, making sure you squeeze out all the juices from the almonds in the sieve. Transfer to the fridge to set for 3–4 hours.

Meanwhile, make the poached apricots. In a wide, deep saucepan, make a syrup by bringing the water, sugar and lemon zest to the boil. Simmer for a few minutes, then add the prepared fruit. Cover with a cartouche (see p 255) and leave to simmer for 20–40 minutes, until the fruit is soft and translucent. If you want a denser syrup, remove the fruit pieces from the pan using a slotted spoon and boil the syrup for a few more minutes until reduced to the desired thickness. Set the fruit and syrup aside to cool.

To serve, turn out the *Panna Cottas* from their moulds onto serving plates and serve with the poached apricots.

Toasted Fig Leaf *Panna Cotta*

Fig leaves have a flavour and scent somewhere between tree sap, desiccated coconut and a freshly picked green fig. It's a mellow flavour that is coaxed out by a light toasting in the oven. These toasted leaves lend a warm, grassy, July-dusk flavour to a delicate *Panna Cotta*.

Fig leaves are surprisingly easy to find. Fig trees grow wild all over the countryside around me in Sardinia, and I have seen them in London too, in public parks and alongside canals.

Makes 6 small *Panna Cottas*

flavourless oil, for oiling the moulds
4 fig leaves, washed and torn
2 gelatine leaves (3–4 g)
400 ml (13 fl oz/generous 1½ cups) cream
100 ml (3½ fl oz/scant ½ cup) milk
50 g (2 oz) sugar
macerated blackberries or other poached summer fruit, to serve

Lightly oil 6 dariole or similar-size *Panna Coctta* moulds.

Preheat the grill and lay out the fig leaves on a baking sheet. With the door open, and half an eye on them, lightly toast the fig leaves for a few minutes, until they begin to smell good and toasty. Remove from the oven.

Slake the gelatine in a small bowl of cold water until softened (see p 259).

Meanwhile, gently heat the cream, milk and sugar in a saucepan.

Add the toasted fig leaves to the warming milk mixture, scrunching the leaves with your hands as you drop them into the pan. When the mixture comes to the boil remove from the heat and set aside to infuse for 3–4 minutes.

Remove the gelatine from the soaking water and squeeze it in your hands to remove as much excess water as you can. Add the gelatine to the warm cream mixture and stir well to dissolve (make sure the cream is warm enough to melt the gelatine).

Strain the mixture through a fine sieve into a jug, discarding the solids in the sieve. Pour the mixture evenly into the prepared moulds then transfer to the fridge to chill for at least 4 hours before serving.

To serve, turn out the *Panna Cottas* from their moulds onto serving plates and serve with macerated blackberries or other poached summer fruit.

Cappuccino *Panna Cotta* with Espresso Caramel

In the late 15th century, Queen Isabella of Spain boasted that she had only bathed twice in her entire life. Based on this, my grandmother used to refer to anything beige or pale brown as 'Isabella-coloured', in reference to the unwashed Queen. I cannot make these Cappuccino *Panna Cottas* without thinking about this description, or my granny herself, as it was she that gave me my very first taste of coffee. Coffee is a natural flavour for a *Panna Cotta*, as it pairs so well with cream, and the espresso caramel which is drizzled over the top is a deliciously sweet, bitter and smoky addition (and very easy to make).

Makes 6 small (dariole-sized) or 4 larger *Panna Cottas*

150 ml (5 fl oz/scant ⅔ cup) espresso
100 ml (3½ fl oz/scant ½ cup) milk
50g (2 oz) Demerara sugar
2 gelatine leaves (3–4 g)
200 ml (7 fl oz/scant 1 cup) cream

For the caramel

80 g (3 oz/⅓ cup) sugar
40 ml (3 tbsp) water
40 ml (3 tbsp) espresso
pinch of salt

Warm the espresso, milk and sugar in a small saucepan and bring the mixture just to a simmer, stirring occasionally to dissolve the sugar. Remove from the heat.

Meanwhile, slake the gelatine in a small bowl of cold water until softened (see p 259).

Squeeze as much liquid from the softened gelatine as you can, then add it to the still-hot coffee mixture, whisking well to dissolve the gelatine.

Add the cream to the mixture and whisk well. Pour evenly into the prepared moulds/darioles (or espresso cups for extra kitsch-ness), then transfer to the fridge for at least 4 hours to set.

For the caramel sauce, in a small saucepan bring the sugar and water to the boil, swirling the pan occasionally to help the sugar dissolve. Cook over a high heat, keeping an eye on it and swirling occasionally for a few minutes until the syrup has turned to a caramel colour, and begun to smell of caramelised sugar.

Turn the heat down to low, pour in the coffee and whisk well (take care, as the mixture will bubble up at this point). Add the salt and whisk gently until the syrup is completely smooth. Leave to cool. To serve, drizzle a small amount of the coffee caramel over the *Panna Cotta*.

Note

You can make the caramel sauce a few days in advance and store it covered in the fridge. It is also good with vanilla ice cream. This *Panna Cotta* is especially good with some extra double (heavy) cream, and then the coffee caramel over the top, for gentle overkill.

Green Lemon Posset

A posset is even easier to make than a *Panna Cotta* and just as delightful to eat. A little denser, a little more intense, its richness is undercut by the lip-smacking acidity of lemon. The texture is something quite lovely, like mascarpone, with the same thickness as soured cream. As I find it difficult to buy good, thick cream here, a posset feels like a wonderful way of entrapping the best of Italian citrus in a pudding that is peculiarly British.

Happily, the lemon season here in Sardinia seems to last all year, depending on which variety is grown, and in my communal garden green lemons last all through the summer and into early autumn. They have a wonderful fresh, unripe flavour, much like a lime.

Makes 6 small possets

- 450 ml (15 fl oz/1¾ cups) double (heavy) cream
- 90 g (3¼ oz/½ cup) sugar
- 80 ml (2½ fl oz/5 tbsp) green lemon juice (around 2–3 large lemons) and the finely grated zest from the lemons (see introduction)

Put the cream and sugar in a medium saucepan and bring to a low boil. Stir gently and continue to boil for a couple of minutes.

Remove from the heat and allow to cool for 5 minutes.

Add the lemon juice and zest to the cream mixture, then strain the mixture into a jug (discard the zest) and pour evenly into small tea cups or espresso cups (a little goes a long way). Leave to chill in the fridge for at least 2 hours, or overnight.

Serve with the semolina shortbread on page 44.

Note

This is also very good with poached blackberries and sage from the chocolate tart recipe on page 54.

Note

If you want to replicate the flavour of green lemons, use 3 normal lemons and 1 lime.

VIA
CAN. LUIGI
MATTA

Poached Peaches with Rose Geranium & Vermentino

There are peaches that are made to be eaten, *subito*, preferably over the sink, and then there are other peaches that are a little firmer, still with a fine scent, but less yielding – and these are peaches for poaching. I used to be indifferent to poached fruit, because I mistakenly thought it was served hot, and to my mind the only place for hot fruit is steaming inside a pie or skulking under a crumble. But actually the true joy of good poached fruit is that it is served cold, and so is a wonderfully cool, clean, fresh way to finish a meal.

There is no denying that cold cooked fruit, soft and giving but firm enough to hold its shape, served in a light, translucent, fragrant syrup, is also reminiscent (in the best way) of tinned fruit. Tinned peaches, which were a treat when I was a child, have a lot of charm. These peaches taste like a refined version of those tinned peaches. The syrup is the prettiest blush pink, and the rose geranium leaves lend a hint of citrus alongside the blowsy musk of rose too. Served with ricotta ice cream (see the recipe for Ricotta & Fig Ripple Gelato on page 204), or simply with some cream, (either mascarpone or softly whipped) they make a very elegant and delicious summer sweet. The whole plate is impossibly pretty.

If you can find the smaller doughnut peaches, then poach these instead and keep them whole, as photographed.

Serves 6–8

- 500 ml (17 fl oz/2 cups) Vermentino di Sardegna or similar dry white wine
- 2 strips of lemon zest
- 150 g (5 oz/⅔ cup) sugar
- 100 ml (3½ fl oz/scant ½ cup) water
- 6–8 ripe peaches, washed
- 4–5 rose geranium leaves, plus geranium petals or leaves to garnish (optional)
- ricotta ice cream (see introduction) or mascarpone, to serve

Put the wine, lemon zest, sugar and water in a wide, deep saucepan and bring to the boil. Turn down to a simmer.

Cut the washed peaches in half and carefully remove the stones trying to leave the halves nicely intact. Place the halves into the syrup and cover with a cartouche (see p 255). Allow to simmer gently for 7–10 minutes, until the peaches are soft. Remove the peaches with a slotted spoon and place them in a dish. Peel away the skins and discard.

Place the poaching liquor back on the heat and simmer to reduce for 3–5 minutes, to form a nice syrupy liquid. Set aside to cool slightly, and then add the geranium leaves, scrunching them a little in your hands before dropping them in to release their scent.

Allow the syrup to cool completely. Once it is cool, strain out the leaves and lemon zest (discard) and pour it over the peaches. Serve the peaches with their syrup and a scoop of ice cream or mascarpone. Scatter over some geranium petals or leaves, if using.

Quince, Bay, Marsala & Hazelnut Trifle
A kind of *Zuppa Inglese*

All things must end and so if they must, then let it be with trifle. Trifle is one of the most pleasurable of all puddings and the most sensual of sweets by the spoon. Layers of soft creaminess sinking finally into the gentle mattress-bounce of moist cake, the irresistible coupling of cream and custard and the light lilt of booze in the background; this is a pudding to rival *Tiramisù* (and for some, to surpass it too).

Zuppa Inglese, or the wonderfully named English Soup, which I have encountered here in Sardinia and seen all over Italy, is disputably an Italian interpretation of England's infamous custard and cake combination, though its origins are (unsurprisingly) hotly debated. Some argue for Naples as its birthplace, sometime around the 19th century, others for Emilia-Romagna or Tuscany. Either way this wonderfully named sweet pops up all over Italy, in all sorts of guises.

This version, which leans more towards a traditional English trifle (no meringue, chocolate or Alchermes) is a celebration of late autumn coming into winter, and the *mela cotogna* (quince) which are happily as at home in Italy as they are in England.

Cooked long and slow as in this recipe, the colours of the quince change miraculously from pale gold to garnet and the fruit becomes intensely floral and fudgy. The combination with the cream, custard and cake topped with the toasted crunch of the nuts and the smoky, Marsala-soaked sponge is a hard one to beat. It takes time to make, but it is worth it. It is no trifling matter.

Feeds 10 modest trifle-eaters, 8 trifle fiends

For the sponge layer

1 × *Pan di Spagna* (see Fatless Sponge, p 238), or use one shop-bought pandoro/boudoir biscuits or trifle sponges

For the custard

600 ml (20 fl oz/2½ cups) double (heavy) cream
100 ml (3½ fl oz/scant ½ cup) whole milk
1 vanilla pod (bean), split
6 egg yolks
100 g (3½ oz/½ cup) sugar

If making your own sponge, follow the recipe on pages 238–239.

Make the custard . Bring the cream, milk, and vanilla pod to a scald in a deep saucepan (see p 256). In a large heatproof mixing bowl, whisk the yolks with the sugar. Once at a scald, pour the milk mix into the egg yolk mixture in a steady stream, whisking all the time. Return the mixture to the pan and place over a medium heat.

Stir constantly, cooking the custard until it is thick enough to coat the back of a wooden spoon. Once thick, strain through a sieve into a container and cover the surface with cling film (plastic wrap). Allow to cool completely. Leave in the fridge until ready to use.

For the quinces, peel and core the fruit, cutting them into quarters and then eighths. (Reserve the peel for the poaching process, which will enhance their ruby colour. You can remove it at the end.)

Put the water, sugar, lemon peel and bay leaves in a deep pan and add the quinces (and bits of peel). Bring to a simmer and cover with a cartouche (see p 255). Poach over a low heat, checking occasionally, for up to 2 hours or more, until the quinces have turned a deep ruby red. Set aside and leave to cool.

For the quinces

3 large quinces (around 650 g/1 lb 7 oz)
350 ml (12 fl oz/1½ cups) water
150 g (5 oz/⅔ cup) sugar
a few strips of lemon peel
2 bay leaves

To finish

350 ml (12 fl oz/1½ cups) double (heavy) cream
150 ml (5 fl oz/scant ⅔ cup) Marsala or sherry
2 tbsp icing (confectioner's) sugar
40g (1½ oz) hazelnuts, lightly toasted and roughly chopped
dark chocolate, grated (optional)

Whip the cream with the icing sugar to soft peaks and set aside.

Now assemble the trifle. Cut the sponge into thick lengths or fingers (large enough to be interesting, small enough to allow space in the bowl for plentiful custard) and place in the centre of your trifle bowl/dish. Sprinkle over the Marsala or sherry, and some of the quince juice too, if you like, but don't soak the sponge too much – it's nicer with some cakey body left in it rather than sadly sodden.

Lay over the quinces, then the custard, and finally the cream. Top with the toasted hazelnuts and a grating of dark chocolate, as a nod to the *Zuppa Inglese*, if you wish.

Serve, with aplomb.

Note

If you can't find quinces, then use pears instead, and cut down the poaching time to about 40 minutes, with half the quantity of water.

FORBIDDEN FRUIT

'This special feeling towards fruit, its glory and abundance, is I would say universal. We respond to strawberry fields or cherry orchards with a delight that a cabbage patch or even an elegant vegetable garden cannot provoke.'

— **Jane Grigson**

I remember my grandmother telling me a story about bananas. It was during the Second World War, and she and her brother were given two sacred, smuggled bananas by their parents. Importing of foreign fruit had been banned in 1940, so for years they had merely dreamt of bananas – of banana sandwiches and banana custard, of fried bananas in butter and brown sugar, of bananas and black treacle and cream. Here, at last, were the real fruits, a solid weight held in their hands, their waxy yellow skin at once so familiar and so alien, their tropical perfume reminiscent of another world, impossibly far away. They ate them slowly, just as they were, then draped the empty skins over their bedposts, so they could smell that heady scent as they drifted off to sleep.

I could write an entire book about fruit (if only I could!). There is something so magical about it – the feelings it provokes, the poetry it inspires, the nostalgia it awakens. Fruit is designed to tempt – a plant's ploy to entice us animals to eat it and thus spread its seed as far as possible. Fruit develops from flowers, an obvious fact botanically perhaps, but when you consider the life cycle of a plant it is impossible not to be bewitched by the reality that from one of nature's most beautiful manifestations is born another.

There are fruit trees in our shared garden where I live in Sardinia. The pomegranates have been the most extraordinary to watch develop through the year. Their flowers, which bloom in May, are a livid vermilion, their petals delicate and frilled, and at the base is a tiny, waxy and spherical shell with its pointed star that will shed its petals and swell to become a pomegranate.

Pomegranates, like so many other fruits here in Italy, were the stuff of myths to me growing up in rural England. I'd never seen one before working in restaurants in London. Like the apple, they have acquired a mythical symbolism, being portrayed in art and literature throughout the centuries, and becoming a symbol of fecundity. Their Italian name, *melagrana*, echoes their shapely similarity to an apple, or *mela*.

The first pomegranates of the year are pale gold, just tinged with pink, and rose-tainted seeds inside that are mouth-puckeringly sharp. The skin develops to a darker pink, and the seeds to a bright

and glassy crimson, as they become ever-more sweet towards Christmas. They are a gift to cooks and artists, their honeycomb interiors bedecked with bright jewels just begging to be portrayed in paint or prised open and eaten messily.

Here in Sardinia I have encountered many different ways to eat them. Each person has their own particular method for the fiddly extraction of the seeds from the bitter, papery white membrane, and each person their own way of eating them too, though most people I know chew the seeds and then spit them out rather than swallow the hard white nib.

Growing up, I remember wonderful fruit, but it was always English, often sour and almost always eaten with copious sugar. My mum grew strawberries and raspberries, which we licked and dipped in sugar for tea, or ate with cream and sugar on Sundays, and rhubarb and apples and gooseberries, which were stewed with plenty of sugar too. Peaches and apricots – these came from a tin in suspiciously clear syrup.

Thus, the ripeness and abundance of Italian fruit provides me with great daily pleasure and awe, whether it be shopping for it, eating it, spying it growing through gates or admiring it overhanging garden walls. Throughout each season, fresh, seasonal fruit is piled high in great crates in the market with a carelessness and copiousness that never ceases to fill me with wonder. During my weekly market shop we, the throng of thrifty shoppers (of which I am easily the youngest by 30 years and tallest by 30 cm) push and prod our way through careless tumbles of it, squeezing, sniffing, tapping and tasting. 'Are these Sardinian?' the tiny lady next to me demands, presenting a dusky plum for inspection. 'As Sardinian as I am,' the vendor replies, without a second's hesitation.

The drupe family – stone fruit such as apricots, plums and peaches – are particularly glorious, larger, sweeter and more complex than anything I ever dreamt of in England. In late summer the peaches reach the size of small melons, and jostle for space next to miniature watermelons zig-zagged and striped with various shades of sci-fi green. The vendors cut a scarlet slice with a pocket-knife and hand it to me to confirm its sweetness. 'Tap a watermelon and if it sounds hollow, it's ripe,' one vendor tells me. I rap my knuckles on one. 'There's no one inside!' laughs another.

One of the most extraordinary things about fruit in Italy is its abundance. The sunshine that appears in such timid and fretful bursts in England exists here in such an unmeasured quantity that it breeds fruit which is large, juicy, sweet and ripe, and bountiful to the point of embarrassment. Fruit that for me would seem an enormous luxury is an everyday reality for every Italian, and like many other aspects of Italian food culture it is utterly egalitarian. It costs very little, and near where I live in Oristano fruits such as melons grow so easily they are even fed to animals as fodder. One of the strangest things I have ever stumbled across is a field of Sardinian sheep at dusk, daintily eating discarded watermelons.

Apart from the size, sweetness and abundance, another thing that never ceases to astonish me is the riot of colour the fruit here provides. Only heat and sun could produce such lavish shades, next to which the muted English tones of russet apples and conference pears pale in comparison. The loud scarlet shout of a watermelon slice, the dappled amber of a good apricot, flecked with pink; the luminous interiors of *fichi d'india*. These extraordinary fruits (known also as prickly pears) grow wild all over Sardinia and are harvested in the late summer or early autumn, using a length of cane that is split at one end to skewer the spiny specimens from a safe distance.

Prickly pears are traditionally eaten after a large meal to celebrate *Ferragosto*, a national holiday in Italy that falls on 15th August. I love the way different fruits mark the arrival of specific seasons and festivals. Here in Sardinia, as imported fruit is still a relative novelty, fruit is only available and eaten within its season. The rituals of an edible calendar are deeply comforting, and mean there is always something to look forward to. I map my life by the market, and measure my year in fruit and vegetables. *Nespole* (loquats) mark the beginning of the stone fruits and thus the summer, and prickly pears mark the end of this long, seemingly never-ending season, which lasts the best part of six months, from May to November. Late summer brings figs and peaches, then autumn heralds the arrival of pears and apples; by November the citrus begins, and this keeps us going all through the winter until the *nespole* appear again, alongside sweet spring strawberries.

Another phenomenon I have come to relish about Italian life is that of eating fruit on the beach. In high summer, when the whole of Sardinia (or Oristano, at least) decamps to the beach, it is customary to take a little cool-box packed with ripe fruit still dewy with fresh water from a recent rinsing. After a few hours swimming and sunning ourselves we reach for a downy peach, a dusky plum or a juicy wedge of watermelon. The intense heat, the salty air and the sight of the glittering sea ahead make this one of the most perfect ways to enjoy fruit, and something I somehow can't imagine recreating on damp holidays in Dorset.

Watermelons are one of the highlights of high summer in Sardinia. It's a fruit I had previously dismissed as watery and flavourless until I tasted them here. Figs, too, provide fresh joy every August and September. They grow wild all over the countryside, both the white (green) and black (purple) varieties, and split and explode as the heat and lack of rain becomes unbearable, exposing their shocking scarlet, Georgia O'Keeffe interiors.

The real glory of figs, as Elizabeth David wrote, is that 'no two are ever the same, which makes the perfect one far to seek'. I eat a hundred figs every summer, forever hopeful to find perfection, and just occasionally, I hit upon it. It is no great hardship to consume 70 or so imperfect specimens in the hunt for excellence. The white (or pale green) variety are my favourite, more juicy and jammy inside and with a taste more reminiscent of rain than the later, black, drier and more coconutty ones.

Ices, slices and endings

In Sardinia, as in all of Italy, meals culminate in fruit. It is an integral part of daily eating, and of every meal. Whatever is in season, or looks good at the market (after much prodding, tapping, sniffing, tasting and plenty of accusations of price inflation), is washed and plonked on the table with the nonchalance only a nation blessed with such natural wonders could demonstrate.

In peak summer the fruit is served on ice, which makes it somehow that much more glamorous and special. It is amazing what a difference such small things can make, but eating an iced grape or slice of melon can feel like the most joyous thing to those of us used to a more temperate climate, where most of our fruit comes ready chilled by the surrounding air or shop shelves. Perhaps iced fruit could fill the gap left by the sad (but inevitable) fate of the fruit salad.

Fresh fruit truly is the most delicious end to any meal. The seasons provide the perfect complement to the corresponding main course; the rich ragus and creamy pastas of midwinter cut through by a tart clementine, or in summer the salty fat of a barbecued sausage cleansed by icy-cold melon. However, as this is after all a book of pudding and not a book of fruit, I would always argue for the place for pudding. After fruit comes coffee, and with coffee comes *dolci*. For everyday meals, fruit is the perfect closure, but for special occasions, Sundays and celebrations, a bit of pudding is called for.

Equally, one of the best reasons to make sorbets and granitas, or ices, is to capture the fleeting flavour of fruit in a new and delicious way. Sorbets and granitas allow you to add new flavours to fruit bases, and to enjoy the same icy fruit flavours in a different textural format. For recipes see Gelato (see p 174–213).

Drunken peaches

Another way to turn good fruit into an instant pudding is to put peach slices into the remainder of your glass of red wine. As it will no doubt be summer (when the peaches are ripe) you will be drinking your red wine chilled, and this cool and refreshing combination provides the perfect ending.

Red Wine Roasted Figs

I am always looking for new ways to use figs, as they grow wild all over Sardinia and are too prolific to eat raw all at once. The red wine highlights the inherent winey flavour of the fruit and creates a delicious figgy syrup in the oven. This is a very low-maintenance pudding which you could serve with the Rosemary *Fior di Latte* on page 208, with ricotta or mascarpone cream, or alternatively as a sort of cheese course, with a fresh goat's cheese, a tangy pecorino or blue cheese.

Serves 4

8 small black figs
1 tbsp sugar
1 small glass of red wine

Preheat the oven to 180°C (350°F/Gas 4). Lay the figs in a single layer in the bottom of a small baking dish. Cut the woody stalk off the tips of the figs, then slit them in not-quite quarters (they should still be intact at their bases).

Sprinkle over the sugar and pour over the glass of wine.

Bake in the oven for 20–25 minutes.

Remove and leave to cool a little before serving.

Roast Stuffed Peaches with Almond Crumble

Towards August the Italian peaches swell to the size of small melons, and the gradation of colours on their skin rivals the most exquisite painting: blush pink, speckles of gold and scarlet dimples, saffron yellow. They usually have their papery-green leaves and stalk still attached, which gives me enormous pleasure, hailing as I do from a land where peach trees are an impossibility. The fruit's heady smell so redolent of summer, their downy cheeks peaking through the brown paper bag. Peaches and cream, peaches to dream.

The best way to eat a ripe peach is, of course, on the beach, with the sun in your eyes and the juice dripping down your wrists. That is the time for perfect peaches. For firmer specimens, this is a perfect recipe, which is worth making for the smell alone. It is also a rather wonderful way of making individual fruit crumbles: each peach is a perfect portion.

Serves 8

4 firm but fragrant peaches
80 g (3 oz) amaretti biscuits
30 g (1 oz) whole almonds (unblanched or blanched)
1 tbsp Demerara sugar
30 g (1 oz) butter
30 g (1 oz/¼ cup) 00 or plain (all-purpose) flour
pinch of salt
zest of ½ a lemon

To finish

small glass of Amaretto (optional)
mascarpone, to serve

Preheat the oven to 170°C (340°F/Gas 3).

Rinse and dry the peaches and cut them in half. Remove and discard the stones.

Blitz all of the remaining ingredients together in a blender. (If you don't have a blender, crush the biscuits by hand, chop the almonds and rub everything together in a bowl as if you were making a crumble mixture.) Once you have a camel-brown crumb, take walnut-sized pieces of mixture in your hand and squeeze, forming 8 rough balls. Press each ball into the hole of each peach half to create a false stone.

Place the peaches in a baking dish and sprinkle over the Amaretto (if using). Transfer to the oven and bake for up to 1 hour, until the peaches are just brown, and slightly shrivelled inside their now ill-fitting jackets. They should be tender when tested with the tip of a knife.

Allow to cool slightly, then serve with a glass of Amaretto, if you like. This is also good served with a blob of mascarpone.

Tiramisù

Originally dreamt up in Treviso and now beloved beloved all over Italy and for good reason, this is my perfect pick-me-up.

I like to make mine in a gratin dish or trifle bowl for serving by the generous scoopful, rather than in individual portions. If you wish to make it in a big trifle bowl such as the one in the photo, just double the quantities.

Serves 4 greedy people or 6 ascetics

- 3 eggs, separated
- 100 g (3½ oz/½ cup) caster (superfine) sugar
- 500 g (1 lb 2 oz) mascarpone
- 200 ml (7fl oz/scant 1 cup) strong black coffee
- 80 ml (5 tbsp) Marsala
- 20 ml (1½ tbsp) brandy
- 20–24 Savoiardi biscuits or ladyfinger biscuits
- 5 tbsp cocoa (unsweetened chocolate) powder, for dredging

Put the egg yolks and sugar in a mixing bowl and whisk using an electric beater (or a stand mixer) until thick, pale and mousse-like.

Mix in the mascarpone by hand, folding it in until completely incorporated. Make the coffee (make sure it is good, strong, espresso coffee). Stir the Marsala and brandy into the coffee and set aside in a shallow bowl.

In a separate, clean bowl using clean beaters, whisk the egg whites until smooth, creamy peaks are formed, but not too stiff so that they become dry. Fold into the mascarpone mixture, incorporating them gently so as not to lose too much air.

Dunk the Savoiardi/ladyfinger biscuits briefly into the coffee mixture, making sure they are fully immersed, and arrange them on the base of your trifle dish/bowl. The idea is not to have them either sopping or still-crisp, but somewhere in between. I dip, hold for a second, turn and hold for another second, and then remove. It pays to be a little OCD here, as no one wants a *Tiramisù* swimming in liquid.

Scoop the first half of the mascarpone mixture over the Savoiardi layer. Spread out evenly. Repeat the soaked-Savoiardi layer and then finish with the second mascarpone layer on top of this. Dredge well with cocoa powder and place in the fridge to set for 1–2 hours. If you prefer, you can add fresh cocoa powder just before serving; I like it when it has slightly melted into the cream.

Whipped Coffee & Ricotta Instant Mousse

Based on a much-loved and oft-imitated recipe from Elizabeth David's *Italian Food*, which was the only cookbook I had with me when I arrived in Sardinia, and which my grandmother had given to me when I graduated from cooking school. This is one of those dishes that, like all of Elizabeth David's recipes, has stood the test of time. It feels somehow timeless, and is incredibly simple to produce and utterly delicious to eat. The combination of ricotta and coffee is one of my favourites – the bitter, burnt edge of coffee pairs so well with the unapologetically sweet-cheesiness of ricotta. I add a dash of Marsala because I use it in my *Tiramisù*, so I always have it hanging about, and it's woodiness works brilliantly with coffee. You can add rum (David's suggestion) or brandy or Amaretto as you see fit.

I like to serve it in little glass bowls with a light dusting of toasted hazelnut and dark chocolate on the top.

If you want to make this into a more substantial and fancy pudding you can layer it up in glasses with some crushed biscuits or soaked trifle sponges in between. I would suggest *Amaretti* or the *Cantucci* on pages 27 and 28.

Serves 3–4

150 ml (5 fl oz/scant ⅔ cup) double (heavy) cream
250 g (9 oz) ricotta
3 tbsp icing (confectioner's) sugar
2 tbsp strong espresso coffee
2 tsp Marsala
crushed amaretti or cantucci biscuits (optional)

To decorate

10 g (½ oz) dark chocolate
handful of toasted hazelnuts

Whisk the cream to form soft peaks in a mixing bowl. Set aside.

Whisk the ricotta and icing sugar in a separate bowl until smooth. Add the coffee and Marsala, and whisk until incorporated. Fold the cream into the ricotta mixture.

Spoon into your chosen serving vessels (layering with biscuits if you wish) and chill in the fridge for at least 2 of hours before serving.

To serve, grate the chocolate over the top and sprinkle with the toasted hazelnuts.

QUANTO BASTA

or
As much as is enough.

The Goldilocks porridge quantity, QB: anyone who cooks in Italy will know all about the phenomenon of *quanto basta,* which means any and all of the following;

as much as is enough
as needed
as required
just enough
the right amount

Charming, wise, practical, elusive, enigmatic and infuriating in equal measure, it is also the invariable response given by any serious Italian home cook when I ask feebly for the precise amount of lard, oil, sugar, egg, butter they are adding to their biscuit/pastry/tart/cake mix. It is the home cook's finger-wagging way of saying there is no such thing as perfect precision and searching for it is fruitless, foolish and downright deluded.

When I cook with my friend Loredana, she becomes vocally furious if I ask for precise measurements.She explains that the ingredients are never exactly the same, so how can the measurements possibly be so? The almonds are sometimes drier, sometimes fresher and therefore juicer, and so the amount of egg white needed to make a good paste for *amaretti* will vary accordingly.

Loredana measures by eye, and pours enough in as feels right to her. She scoffs at my notepad and pencil, at my digital scales, at my obsession with these ridiculous 'grams'. She says, peering wryly at me over her spectacles, that I may merrily write what I like, but no one's *amaretti* will be exactly the same; that she learned the recipe from her mother-in-law and made the biscuits with her, and then watched her make them many times, but even so *her* biscuits taste and look completely different.

It is not only the ingredients that count, she says, but also *la mano* (the hand). Her mother-in-law was blessed with *mani d'oro* (golden hands – also a popular name for beauty salons and hairdressers in Italy) and so her *amaretti* always came out perfectly, and, try as Loredana might, she will never be able to replicate them exactly. This does not stop her making them, or stop hers from being delicious too. In fact it is one of the marvellous (and infuriating) things about cooking, that whatever you do, however hard you try, no two dishes will ever taste exactly the same.

Of course, no recipe can be perfectly precise, and there are always environmental factors that will vary and affect the finished result. In an ideal world we would all make and know these recipes as often and as well as Loredana does, meaning that we too could judge everything by eye. But the world is far from ideal, and most of us must make do with measurements, despite Loredana's grumblings of disapproval.

As much as I have been tempted to include instructions with QB, I have avoided it, as I know how frustrating it may be for those of us cooking at home and in a rush. Even so, it is a brilliant and beguiling part of life in Italy, and a sort of wry Italian philosophy for living: *We must do as much as is enough*.

Campari Spritz Jelly

I don't make jelly often. In fact, I'm not sure I've ever made one before this, but there is something about jelly that is hugely happy-making, and bringing it wobbling to a table especially so.

The violent colour of this particular jelly is especially pleasing, and it has the same bittersweetness as a Spritz, which means it matches well with a simple creamy gelato, like the Mascarpone Ice Cream on page 192.

I use one of my bundt tins to make a spectacular big jelly, but if you want to make individual portions in smaller containers, you can.

Makes 1.4 litres (48 fl oz) jelly mould or 8–9 small individual jellies

flavourless oil, for oiling the mould
1 bottle (750 ml) prosecco
150 g (5 oz/⅔ cup) sugar
2–3 strips of orange zest
20 g (¾ oz) leaf gelatine
70 ml (2½ fl oz/⅓ cup) Campari
juice of 2 large oranges (about 160 ml/5½ fl oz/⅔ cup; blood orange is best for colour)
creamy gelato of choice, to serve (see introduction)

Lightly oil the jelly mould(s) using a pastry brush.

In a large saucepan, gently warm 200 ml (7 fl oz/scant 1 cup) of the prosecco with the sugar and orange zest until the sugar has dissolved. Set aside.

Slake the gelatine in cold water for 1 minute until soft (see p 259), then squeeze it to remove any excess water and put it in the saucepan with the (still hot) prosecco and sugar. Whisk well to dissolve.

Add the remainder of the prosecco, the Campari and the orange juice. Stir well, then strain through a sieve (discard the zest) and pour into the jelly mould (or moulds, if making small individual jellies). Leave to set overnight in the fridge.

To turn out of the mould, fill a large bowl with hot water, hold the mould inside for a few seconds to warm the jelly and help release the sides, then invert onto a plate.

Serve with a scoop of gelato.

5

YEASTED AND FRIED

If I had to choose just one category of sweet things, this would be the one I'd save. I've talked about my love of buns at great length elsewhere, but I feel the need to repeat that brioches, buns and doughnuts are to me the greatest sweet things of all, because they combine two of my favourite things – bread and cake – into one sweet, pillowy wonder-food.

Let them eat brioche…

Interestingly, Marie Antoinette's oft-quoted phrase is actually more accurately translated as 'let them eat brioche' (*Qu'ils mangent de la brioche*). A brioche *is* almost a cake, enriched as it is with butter, sugar and usually eggs too. Because of the added fats (most brioche recipes call for milk as well) the crumb of a brioche is very cakey: close-textured and bouncy. The true appeal of brioche is that it manages to combine the best of both worlds. It is both cake and bun at once: the perfect hybrid, the perfect union.

Brioche col Tuppo, the classic brioche of Sicily, is slightly less sweet and rich than some brioche recipes, and a little lower in eggs and butter too, as it is designed to be eaten with (sweet and creamy) gelato.

Fritta è buona anche una ciabatta
'Even a slipper is good deep-fried'

It is a truth universally acknowledged that anything deep-fried is delicious. Deep-fried enriched doughs (like *Bomboloni*) are some of the most delicious things of all. Deep-frying the dough (rather than baking it as you would for a standard brioche/bun) means that it remains extremely moist and *squidgy* (a highly technical word), as all the moisture is trapped within, rather than evaporating in an oven. In addition, the frying oil slightly penetrates the dough, giving it that irresistible greasiness which leaves a sheen on lips, hands and fingers, and tell-tale stains on paper bags.

Flours

When making enriched doughs, it is usual to use a mixture of two different flours, as my recipes do. The Manitoba, 0 Flour, or strong bread flour, provides a higher gluten content and makes the dough more elastic, and thus the crumb of the finished brioche more 'bready'. The 00 flour, plain (all-purpose) or 'soft' flour has a low gluten content, making the crumb more 'cakey'.

Bomboloni alla Crema
Doughnuts with Pastry Cream

When I first arrived in Sardinia I couldn't believe the strange but wonderful phenomenon of *Bomboloni* for breakfast. Luca – who'd been deprived of them in London for four years – used to have two of these *crema*-filled doughnuts for breakfast every day to compensate.

A *Bombolone*, or a *Bomba* as it is sometimes known, is what we would call a doughnut – a fried sweet round of dough dusted with sugar and usually filled to bursting with thick, yellow Italian pastry cream. Deriving their name from their grenade-like shape, the way they burst as you bite into them also provides a suitably explosive echo. Habitually eaten at breakfast with a coffee or occasionally as a *merenda* (snack), they are so popular they are also made in mini format and placed in dainty paper cases, and included when you buy a selection tray of *dolci* to take as a gift.

A sugar-crusted, cream-filled doughnut is the most indulgent way to begin the day.

Makes 5

For the *Bomboloni*

- 60 ml (4 tbsp) milk
- 20 ml (1½ tbsp) water
- 30 g (1 oz) sugar, plus extra to sprinkle
- 7 g (1 generous tsp) fresh yeast
- 250 g (9 oz/2 cups) 00 or plain (all-purpose) flour, plus extra to dust
- 50 g (2 oz) butter, softened
- 2 eggs
- zest of 1 lemon
- 1 tsp salt
- 1 litre (34 fl oz/4 cups) flavourless oil, for deep-frying and for oiling

For the filling

- 1 × batch of Pastry Cream (see p 232)

In a small saucepan, warm the milk to a scald (see p 259), then immediately add the water to bring it back to blood temperature. Once tepid (test with your finger), add the sugar and yeast and whisk to dissolve.

Put all of the remaining ingredients (except for the oil) into a mixing bowl then pour in the yeast liquid and mix well to form a dough. Transfer to a work surface. This dough is quite sticky, but don't add flour – just mix well and allow your hands to get sticky as you knead it for a few minutes, or use an electric mixer with the dough hook attachment.

Once you have a smooth dough (it will be quite wet but you want it stretchy and uniform), lightly oil a clean bowl and place the dough inside. Cover with clingfilm (plastic wrap) or an oiled plastic bag and leave in a warm place to rise for 60–90 minutes (or overnight in the fridge), until doubled in size.

Lightly oil your digital scale and work surface. Scrape out the dough from the bowl onto the oiled surface.

Using a dough scraper, cut small sections from the dough to create 5 × 80 g (3 oz) pieces. Shape them into balls in your hands, circling the palm of your hand around them and then using the scraper to turn them until you create smooth balls (there are also some good YouTube videos demonstrating this).

Yeasted and fried

continued →

continued →

Place the balls in a floured tray (pan) a few inches apart. Cover the tray with oiled clingfilm (plastic wrap) or a tea towel and leave to prove for 60–90 minutes, until doubled in size.

Heat the oil in a large, deep, heavy-based pan (don't fill it more than two-thirds full) to 180°C (350°F). (If you don't have a thermometer, test the temperature of the oil using a small piece of bread. If it browns after 30 seconds in the oil, the oil is ready. If it browns any quicker, the oil is too hot and will need to cool a little before you fry the doughnuts.)

Pick up the doughnuts very gently with your dough scraper, then fry the doughnuts in the hot oil two at a time until ginger biscuit-brown all over, turning to cook evenly (cut one open to check they are cooked through). Drain on a baking sheet lined with absorbent paper, then dust in sugar.

Once they have cooled, pierce a hole in the side of each. Using a piping bag, pipe in the pastry cream until full to bursting.

Serve, with delight.

Note

Digital scales and a probe thermometer are useful for this recipe, as is a dough scraper.

Brioche Col Tuppo

These shining golden buns crowned with small, spherical heads form part of a traditional Sicilian breakfast. The *tuppo* describes a *chignon* or topknot of hair pinned to the top of a woman's head – what in England we would call a bun.

Characterised by their primrose-yellow, perfumed crumb and extreme softness (*sofficissima*), the buns are ideally enjoyed while still warm, either stuffed with balls of rapidly melting gelato or eaten alongside the almond granita that Sicily is famed for.

As is to be expected, the *tuppo* is a source of great delight and occasional torment – seizing and tearing off someone's *tuppo* being the ultimately provocative act (I read somewhere that there is even a hashtag for this: #donttouchmytuppo). The *tuppo* also serves a practical purpose as well as an aesthetic one: once torn away from its soft body it is used to *inzuppare* or soak up the pools of creamy melting gelato/granita. It is the ideal dunking tool.

They take a while to make so they are a good thing to save for a weekend, and then you can either leave the dough overnight to have them ready for a late breakfast, or make them during a day at home to enjoy in the afternoon as an indulgent *merenda* (snack). They are also another wonderful and edible celebration of breasts.

Makes 8

160 ml (5½ fl oz/⅔ cup) milk
1 tsp honey
15 g (½ oz) fresh yeast
2 eggs
400 g (14 oz/3⅓ cups) 0 or strong white flour (see p 247)
100 g (3½ oz/¾ cups) 00 or plain (all-purpose) flour
100 g (3½ oz/½ cup) sugar
10 g (½ oz) salt
100 g (3½ oz) butter, softened
zest of 1 orange
a few drops of vanilla extract (optional)
flavourless oil, for oiling

To finish

1 egg, beaten, to glaze
ice cream or sorbet of choice or coffee, to serve (optional)

In a small saucepan, warm the milk gently to a scald (see p 259). Remove from the heat, then stir in the honey and allow to cool to blood temperature (test with your finger). Once the liquid has reached blood temperature, add the yeast and whisk well to dissolve.

In a large mixing bowl, whisk the eggs, then add the milk/yeast mixture and the remaining ingredients (except the oil). At this point you can transfer the dough to the bowl of a stand mixer with the dough hook attached, if you have one, and mix the dough until it is smooth and elastic.

If you do not have a stand mixer, then work the dough in the mixing bowl with first a spoon and then your hands. It will be very sticky. Mix together until you have an even batter and then scrape it onto a lightly oiled work surface and cover with the bowl. Leave to rest for a few minutes, then uncover and begin to knead the dough until it is smooth and elastic (it will still be quite wet so don't worry if it's sticking. Use a dough scraper to scrape up any bits that stick to the work surface).

Place the dough in a clean, lightly oiled bowl and leave in a warm place to rise until doubled in size, which can take up to 2 hours. (At this stage you can place the dough, covered with clingfilm (plastic wrap) or an oiled plastic bag, in the fridge to rise overnight and come back to it in the morning.)

Once risen, remove the dough from its bowl and cut it into 8 pieces weighing 100 g (3½ oz) each. Lightly oil your scales and work surface. Divide the remaining dough into 8 small even-sized pieces of around 10 g (½ oz) each (which will form the *tuppi*).

Shape all the pieces into rounds. Place them a few inches apart on a large baking tray (pan) lined with baking parchment.

Press two fingers or a thumb firmly into the centre of each of the larger dough balls to create an indentation. Using your fingertips, gently press the smaller ball – the *tuppo* – into the indentation.

Cover the buns with oiled clingfilm and leave in a warm place to rise until doubled in size (this will take 1½ hours, more or less, depending on the temperature of your room).

Preheat the oven to 180°C (350°F/Gas 4).

Brush the tops of the buns all over with the beaten egg and then place them in the oven. Bake for 12–15 minutes until golden.

Serve warm, stuffed with balls of gelato or sorbet, or plain with a coffee; they are sweet and delicious enough to hold their own.

Note

These are slightly larger in size compared to the *Maritozzi* (see p 168), as you need space to accommodate the balls of gelato. Though also a brioche bun, they are very different in texture and flavour. The texture of the crumb is more cakey, and the flavour more buttery and sweet.

BUNS + NUNS

Buns of various shapes and sizes are found all over the world. Almost every culture, every nation, has its own version of an enriched bread, often saved for celebrations. I personally believe (as the Romans do) that every day is a celebration, and that any and every day deserves a bun.

There is something intrinsically celebratory, generous and sensual about buns, about their softness and their satisfyingly spherical shape. For me it seems no coincidence that the word 'abundant' has the word 'bun' sandwiched within it. Perhaps it is specifically their roundness that makes them so appealing, and that undeniably recalls the gentle curves of a breast.

There are countless celebrations of the female breast (and other body parts) in edibles found all over Italy. It is almost impossible to avoid them (one of my most joyous discoveries is a giant, spherical, mozzarella-style cheese complete with tiny teat and known as *la zizzona di Battipaglia'– zizzona* means 'large breast') and they appear particularly often in sweet form.

The connection between sweetness and sensuality goes back to antiquity. Many sweet foods are said to be aphrodisiacs, and the language associated with love is often related to sugar – honeymoons and sweethearts, for example. In Italy, when something/someone is overly sweet, sickly-sweet in a sort of unpleasant way, it is described as *mieloso* or 'honeyed' (from *miele* which means honey). Sharbats, the Arabic icy drink from which sorbet is derived, were considered love potions.

Minne di Sant'Agate are traditional *dolci* from Catania in Sicily, miniature relatives of the *Cassata* (see p 88). They take the form of a woman's breast in homage to Saint Agatha, the patron saint of Catania (and of bakers and breast cancer patients), who was brutally martyred – her breasts removed with pincers – for her devout virginity. Her image is depicted in many paintings showing her holding her breasts on a platter. These little ricotta-filled pastries are one of the typical sweets of Sicily. For another celebration of the female breast in chocolate form, see page 220 for *Capezzoli di Venere*.

The history of confectionery in Italy is inextricably linked to the history of convents, and many traditional Italian *dolci* have their roots in a convent. Along with embroidery, the creation and sale of sweets was a source of revenue (most specifically in Sicily) and a way of keeping the occupants busy.

It seems especially ironic that, having renounced the pleasures of the flesh, the nuns diverted themselves and expressed their creativity by making phallic *Cannoli* and breast-shaped cakes. Competition between convents was fierce, and there is an apocryphal tale of the nuns being

banned by the bishop from the business of making sweets during Holy Week in the 1500s on the grounds that they were so busy baking that they were neglecting their religious duties. One can perhaps see how painting marzipan fruits and shaping cakes into breasts could be more absorbing than praying.

I've always had a weakness for buns. It's the curse of a West Country childhood. Growing up, I was addicted to all buns – the village bakery's Chelsea bun curled into a snail-spiral, the folds concealing the occasional plump and damp raisin, and topped with simple white icing and a glacé (candied) cherry; or the supermarket plain iced bun that came by the half-dozen.

White-iced ones were best (I think the pink ones were flavoured with something pretending to be strawberry): simple oblong milk rolls, impossibly soft and doughy, with a thick bar of sticky white icing on top. The most magical part was their sides, where they had been joined in baking to their neighbours. Once torn apart by impatient fingers, this previously unexposed puffy and pale section was yours for the taking, a hallowed area that was exquisitely, innocently soft, like a baby's cheek.

Cream buns, too, played a part in my childhood. There is a type of bun made in a town near where I grew up that is specific to the area, and is eaten split and filled with cream and jam. Known as a Devonshire split, a Cornish split, or – named after the town itself – a Chudleigh, Elizabeth David talks about these in her *English Bread and Yeast Cookery*. They are small, enriched bread rolls, slightly sweet, simple and bare-faced, split down the middle in a deep smile into which is stuffed abundant cream and jam. The jam is most often a tart scarlet raspberry, the cream almost always the famous clotted cream specific to the West Country.

The first time I visited Rome I discovered an echo of these buns in *Maritozzi*, which are one of my favourite buns (and another example of the link between love/sensuality and sugar) and which I have included a recipe for (see p 168).

Chiacchiere

Carnival in Sardinia means *fritti*. A handful of stalls pop up in the piazza, giant cauldrons of oil bubbling away in the background, the slightly frazzled boys up front, shining delicately with a fine film of fat and frantically handing out grease-stained white paper bags of fresh ring doughnuts and white cardboard trays yielding lengths of *Zippole* (a long, snake-like coil of fried dough perfumed with orange and dusted with sugar). More deliciously and generally made at home and brought as gifts, are the endless trays of *Chiacchiere,* rustling expectantly and silently shedding snowdrifts of icing (confectioner's) sugar as they are passed around the table.

Chiacchiere, 'little gossips' or 'chatter', are a classic sweet of Carnival all over Italy. They are essentially little rags of dough, enriched with a little egg and some alcohol (in Sardinia with the local Vernaccia di Oristano), rolled out thinly, cut in random fashion and then deep-fried and dusted with snowdrifts of icing sugar. The Vernaccia gives them a deliciously almondy note, but if you can't find it you can use sherry, Marsala or Vin Santo, or just plain old white wine. These little, crumbly, crisp, sweet and savoury morsels are deliciously moreish, and known by a number of charming different names including *Bugie* (lies), *Frappe, Cenci* (rags) or *Crostoli.*

You can serve these on their own as a snack, or with coffee, or even better, with little glasses of Vernaccia/Vin Santo and a big bowl of whipped, sweetened mascarpone for communal dunking.

continued →

Makes around 30 (enough for a *festa*)

250 g 00 (9 oz/2 cups) 00
or plain (all-purpose) flour,
plus extra to dust
30 g (1 oz) butter
1 tsp salt
2 tbsp sugar
1 egg, beaten
30 ml (2 tbsp) milk
2 tbsp wine (ideally Vernaccia,
Vin Santo or white wine)
sunflower or other flavourless oil,
for frying
icing (confectioner's) sugar, to dust

Put the flour in a large mixing bowl, add the butter then rub the butter into the flour as if making crumble, until the mixture has a fine sandy texture.

Add the salt and sugar and stir. Then add the egg, milk and the wine to the centre of the mixture and use your hands to bring the mixture together to form a dough (if it looks dry at this point, add a touch more milk).

Transfer to a work surface and knead well for around 5 minutes until smooth. Wrap in clingfilm (plastic wrap) and leave to rest for at least 20 minutes.

Roll out the dough using a rolling pin or pasta machine until around 1 mm thick, as though you were making ravioli, flouring the pasta machine or work surface as needed.

Using a fluted pastry cutter, cut uneven strips of dough. Add a little flour if things start getting sticky.

Heat the oil in a large, deep, heavy-based saucepan (don't fill it more than two-thirds full) to 180°C (350°F). (If you don't have a thermometer, test the temperature of the oil using a small piece of bread. If it browns after 30 seconds in the oil, the oil is ready.) When the oil is ready, begin to fry the *Chiacchiere* a few at a time.

Once evenly brown all over remove them using a slotted spoon and drain on a tray lined with absorbent kitchen paper.

Dust with icing sugar while still warm and then serve.

The *Chiacchiere* keep well in an airtight box for a few days.

Cannoli

The symbolic sweet of Sicily is without doubt the *Cannolo*. Traditionally a Carnival speciality, these crisp, ricotta-filled pastry shells are now eaten all year round all over Italy, and – happily – much loved here in Sardinia too. Many of my Sardinian friends have Sicilian heritage and the *Cannolo*, like so many edible things, has followed on the heels of Sicilian emigrants and found worldwide fame. It seems fitting that they are loved and made here too, as one of the key ingredients in a good *Cannolo* is high-quality sheep's milk ricotta, which is also one of Sardinia's signature products.

Deriving their name from the canes, or lengths of bamboo, which were originally used to shape them (see Note, p 166), *Cannoli* are a classic demonstration of good, simple ingredients put to ingenious use. Creamy, delicate ricotta is essential, as is a good, bitter, dark chocolate. The crumbly crust, or *scorza*, is extra *friabile* due to the addition of lard, and sometimes the shells are still deep-fried in lard too. Of course, if you prefer, you can substitute the lard for butter. Either way, the contrast in textures is an essential part of the enjoyment, the teeth cracking through the crust and then sinking gently into pillowy-soft ricotta cream.

I assumed *Cannoli* would be hard to make, but they are very straightforward. True aficionados will tell you they must be filled at the last minute, to maintain the essential textural contrast, otherwise the shells will become soggy with the absorbed liquid from the ricotta.

Note

The dough can be made well ahead and frozen or kept in the fridge. The shells too can be fried and stored in an airtight container for a couple of days. The filling can also be made a day or two in advance and kept in the fridge.

continued →

Variations

Traditionally *Cannoli* are filled with sweetened ricotta and dark chocolate chips, occasionally with pieces of candied pumpkin stirred through too. I always add a little honey to the filling, as I like the slight woody perfume it gives in contrast to the bitter dark chocolate. Some choose to add chopped candied peel, some vanilla, some decorate with chopped pistachios or glacé (candied) cherries.

Note

Cannoli tubes are very easy to source online, and are also sold in lots of Italian supermarkets and cookware shops. Traditionally, *Cannoli* were shaped around sections of reed cut into lengths and whittled down until smooth. Now the tubes are generally made of stainless steel.

Makes 20 x 10–12 cm (4–5 in) *Cannoli*

For the dough

- 250 g (9 oz/2 cups) 00 or plain (all-purpose) flour
- ½ tsp salt
- 30 g (1 oz) lard or butter, at room temperature
- 1 heaped tbsp honey
- 1 tsp white wine vinegar or lemon juice
- 60 ml (4 tbsp) Marsala
- 1 litre (34 fl oz/4 cups) sunflower or other flavourless oil, for frying

For the filling

- 1 kg (2 lb 4 oz) ricotta (sheep's milk if you can find it), drained
- 180 g (6 oz/¾ cup plus 1 tbsp) sugar
- 4 tsp mild honey
- 120 g (4 oz) dark chocolate (at least 70 per cent cocoa solids), cut into small shards

To decorate

- crushed pistachios
- glacé (candied) cherries
- candied oranges

Line a baking sheet with baking parchment.

To make the dough, put the flour and salt in a large bowl. Add the lard (or butter) and use your fingertips to rub the fat into the flour until the mixture resembles fine breadcrumbs. Add the honey, vinegar or lemon juice and Marsala and mix to form a shaggy dough.

Knead the dough on a work surface for 1–2 minutes until smooth. Wrap in clingfilm (plastic wrap) and set aside to rest for 20 minutes.

Roll the dough (this is easiest using a pasta machine but you can also use a rolling pin) to a 2 mm thickness. Using an upturned pint glass or a round cutter of a similar circumference, cut out 20 circles. Roll the circles with a rolling pin to extend them into long ovals, then roll the ovals over the *Cannoli* tubes. Dip your finger in water and wet the edges to seal them. Place on the prepared baking sheet.

Heat the oil to 180°C/350°F in a large, deep, heavy-based pan (don't fill it more than two-thirds full). If you don't have a thermometer, test the temperature of the oil using a small piece of bread. If it browns after 30 seconds in the oil, the oil is ready. Fry the *Cannoli* a few at a time for about 1 minute, turning occasionally, until sandy brown all over. (Remove the metal tubes while they fry, using tongs, if you can, to ensure the *Cannoli* fry evenly in the middle too.)

Fish them out once they are brown and drain on a baking sheet lined with absorbent paper. Allow to cool completely before filling.

For the filling, beat the ricotta in a bowl with the sugar and honey until smooth and creamy (the sugar will dissolve as you beat). Gently fold the chocolate shards through the cream. Using a table knife, spread the cream into the cooked *Cannoli* tubes, smoothing off each end.

Decorate with crushed pistachios, glacé cherries or slivered candied peel and serve.

Maritozzi

Enriched doughs, by which I mean yeast-risen doughs laced with spices, candied fruit, sugar, eggs, butter or milk, have always been the edible markers of festivities, traditionally baked for high days and holidays. It has always seemed sad to me that buns are seen as suitable only for special occasions. Every day deserves a bun.

Luckily, when in Rome, you can do as the Romans do and have a cream-filled bun, or *Maritozzo*, for breakfast every day, should you wish.

Derived from a spiced bread made during the Middle Ages, these sweet, shining buns were a Lenten treat which included pine nuts, raisins and orange zest, much like a sort of Roman hot cross bun. While we choose to split, toast and butter ours in England, the Romans split and slather theirs abundantly with swathes of whipped cream. Later in their history, the buns became a traditional gift from women to potential suitors, to ensure they became their husbands, or *marito*, hence their name, *Maritozzi*.

This is a two-stage process, but don't be put off; the leaven or sponge is just a kick start for the yeast and only needs half an hour to work, during which time you can weigh up everything else.

Makes 12

For the leaven (sponge)

- 150 ml (5 fl oz/scant ⅔ cup) milk
- 10 g (½ oz) fresh yeast
- 1 tbsp honey
- 60 g (2 oz/½ cup) 00 or plain (all-purpose) flour

For the final dough

- 400 g (14 oz/3¼ cups) 0 or strong white flour (see p 247)
- 100 g (3½ oz/¾ cup, plus 2 tbsp) 00 or plain (all-purpose) flour
- 10 g (½ oz) salt
- 100 g (3½ oz/½ cup) sugar
- 1 egg and 1 egg yolk
- 70 ml (2½ fl oz/5 tbsp) light olive or sunflower oil, plus extra for oiling
- zest of 1 orange
- 100 ml (3½ fl oz/scant ½ cup) water, at room temperature

For the leaven (sponge), warm the milk in a small saucepan (or in the microwave), then transfer to a small bowl and set aside until it is just blood temperature (test it with your finger). Add the yeast, honey and flour to the warm milk and whisk until smooth.

Cover the bowl with clingfilm (plastic wrap) and set aside for 30 minutes. You should see lots of tiny bubbles forming, which means the yeast is working.

For the final dough, in a large mixing bowl, combine the flours and the salt. In a separate bowl mix the sugar, whole egg and egg yolk, oil, orange zest and water. Whisk to mix.

Once the leaven is nice and bubbly add it to the oil and egg mixture, then stir the liquids into the bowl with the flour, bringing it together as a dough with your hands. Knead it on a lightly oiled surface for a few minutes until the dough is smooth. The dough is quite sticky, so use a bread scraper if you have one. (If you have a stand mixer with a dough hook attachment, you can use it to make the dough instead of making it by hand.)

Place the dough in a lightly oiled bowl and cover with cling film. Leave to rise in a warm place until doubled in size, at least 90 minutes (or overnight in the fridge).

Scrape the dough out of the bowl and, using a knife/dough cutter, divide it into twelve 80 g (3 oz) pieces, oiling your scales if necessary.

To finish

1 egg, beaten
2 tbsp runny honey
300 ml (10 fl oz/1¼ cups) double (heavy) cream
3 tbsp icing (confectioner's) sugar, plus extra to dust (optional)

Shape each piece into a neat round (there are good YouTube videos on how to do this) and place them on a baking sheet lined with baking parchment a few inches apart. Cover with an oiled plastic bag or cling film, making sure the bag/film does not touch the surface of the buns.

Leave to prove for 90 minutes (they need to be in a warm and non-draughty spot), until doubled in size. Meanwhile preheat the oven to 190°C (375°F/Gas 5).

Remove the bag/clingfilm from the buns and brush them evenly but gently all over with the beaten egg using a pastry brush.

Transfer to the oven and bake until golden brown and risen, 12–15 minutes.

Using a clean pastry brush, brush them with the honey while still warm. Whip the cream to soft peaks and fold in the icing sugar.

Allow the buns to cool slightly before cutting a deep slit down the middle of each and filling abundantly with whipped cream. They are sometimes then dusted with icing sugar, which you can do if you wish.

Eat, with even more abundant coffee and napkins.

Note

If making these for a special occasion (for Easter or Good Friday, perhaps), you can add raisins and candied peel to the mixture. Add 40 g (1½ oz) raisins and a handful of chopped candied peel to the final dough.

Schiacciata
Sweet Grape Focaccia

A little sweet and a little savoury, this 'squashed' grape bread could happily fit anywhere really, as a breakfast, a *merenda*, or as a summer lunch next to some good cheeses. It is essentially a focaccia dough filled to bursting with sweet grapes, which stain the crumb the most wonderful berry-purple colour.

Originally from Tuscany, *Schiacciata* would traditionally be made with wine grapes after the harvest, but I've made it with cherries, with blueberries and with the elusive *Uva Fragola*, or strawberry grapes (these are best). The fennel seeds add a wonderful aromatic edge, and the crunch of oily, salty bread with a sugared, fennel-scented crust, giving way to a soft, winey interior and the occasional pop of grape and crunch of seed, is truly magical. It's also very good toasted (or warmed in the oven the next day) and eaten with a blob of mascarpone.

It's easiest to make the dough the night before you want to bake the bread, so it can rise in the fridge.

Serves 8–10

7 g fresh yeast or 1 scant tsp of dried
375 ml (13 fl oz/1½ cups) water (at room temperature), plus 10 ml (2 tsp) extra
500 g (1 lb 2 oz/4 cups) 00 or plain (all-purpose) flour
12 g (½ oz) salt
flavourless oil, for oiling
300 g (10½ oz) grapes (or blackberries, blueberries or cherries)
2 tsp fennel seeds, lightly crushed in a pestle and mortar
4–6 tbsp sugar (depending on the sweetness of the fruit)
4 tbsp olive oil
icing (confectioner's) sugar, to dust

Combine the yeast and 375 ml (13 fl oz/1½ cups) water in a mixing bowl. Add the flour to the bowl, mix well, then use your hands to bring the mixture together as a dough. Turn out onto a work surface and knead to form a smooth dough (it will be quite wet). Place the dough in an oiled bowl. (If you have a stand mixer fitted with a dough hook, you can use it to make the dough instead of making it by hand.)

Allow the dough to rest, covered, for 30 minutes.

Add the salt and the extra 10 ml (2 tsp) water and knead into the dough until incorporated. Leave the dough, covered, for another 30 minutes.

After 30 minutes, stretch and fold the corners of the dough, pulling outwards from the base, then tucking the folds over each other. Set aside. Do this once more, 30 minutes later. (This pulling and folding technique builds elasticity in the dough and incorporates air.)

Leave the dough overnight to rise in the fridge, well covered with an oiled plastic bag or cling film (plastic wrap).

The next day, preheat the oven to 190°C (375°F/Gas 5).

Remove the dough and allow it to come up to room temperature. Oil a rectangular baking tray (pan). Divide the dough in half, rolling out each piece into oblongs just shorter than the length of the baking tray. Use oil for the rolling pin and work surface rather than flour.

Place one oblong in the baking tray, then sprinkle over half of the fruit, half of the fennel seeds, half of the sugar and half of the oil.

Place the other oblong of dough on top and press down firmly to seal the two pieces together, spreading the bread out with the palms of your hands to fit the baking tray. Sprinkle over the remaining fruit, fennel seeds and sugar, and drizzle over the remaining oil.

Transfer the baking tray with the bread to the oven and bake for 30 minutes, or until golden and crisp. Allow to cool a bit, then cut into squares, dust with icing sugar and enjoy warm or cool.

6

GELATO

It is impossible to feel anything other than pure unadulterated pleasure when eating ice cream. Ice cream has a power that almost no other food possesses to such a great degree (apart, perhaps, from strings of melted cheese); it makes people happy. Adults, children, grandparents – we all react in the same way when we have a cone or a cup in our hand full of sweet nothings, and melting faster than we can eat it; we all feel good.

Happily, ice cream has always been a big part of my life. Growing up in Devon, and taking many holidays in next-door Cornwall (where it invariably rained all week and we usually either camped in waterlogged campsites or stayed in dank rented cottages) the highpoint of every summer season was ice cream.

There were shacks, sheds or vans near the windswept beaches, our favourites always Kelly's or Willy's, both (supposedly) made in Cornwall. Buttercup-yellow, unceremoniously plonked in a wafer cone and often – if we were lucky – smothered in a layer of clotted cream. Non-holiday ice cream came in a square white tub from the supermarket (often Wall's) and tasted delightfully of sugar and plastic.

When I first tried gelato, I realised this was a completely different thing to the Willy's and Wall's white tubs of my youth. This was something more luxurious, velvety, smoother, lighter, more chewy, and much more glamorous. The display case alone stopped me in my tracks.

An elaborate glass display exhibiting rows of coloured containers enticing passers-by, a man in a black waistcoat scooping the velveteen cream with deft artistry, a stack of real waffle cones on the counter and a riot of colours and flavours to choose from. With its hundreds of lavish colours, curves, crescents and rounded waves of gelato, crowned with shining candied peel, glossy syrup-soaked cherries, crumbled cookies or chips, this was an elaborate opera of ice cream like nothing I'd ever seen.

I first tried such gelato when I was 18 and my granny sent me on an art course in Venice for a few weeks to try to encourage me to absorb some culture. Inevitably, I spent the six weeks skipping lectures and absorbing gelato instead.

After nearly four years in Italy, the love has endured, and I still eat gelato as often as I can.

Gelato, like coffee, pizza, ripe fruit and so many other stalwarts of edible Italian life, is also wonderfully democratic. Unlike so many things that are classified as a 'luxury' (something as purely pleasurable as ice cream must surely be considered a luxury) it is astonishingly cheap, and affordable for everyone.

GELATO VS ICE CREAM: SOME SCIENCE

The main differences between gelato and ice cream are:

1. Gelato rarely contains eggs, whereas most English-style ice cream is based on an egg-enriched frozen custard.
2. Gelato usually has a higher proportion of milk than other ice creams, which contain greater quantities of cream.
3. Gelato contains less air, as it is churned more slowly, so the texture is denser and the flavour is more concentrated.
4. Gelato is served at higher temperatures than ice cream, making it silkily scoop-able.

Many of the gelatos made in modern gelaterias are full of chemicals to achieve the required chewy and smooth texture. Ingredients such as gum arabic, dextrose and carob powder are common. Other gelaterias make their gelato from ready-made powders and mixes. It is not necessary to use all of these powders to create a creamy and delicious gelato, which is one of the reasons for making it at home. The texture will not be exactly the same as those bought in a gelateria, but it will still be very good.

To egg or not to egg

Eggs in ice cream act as stabilisers (they contain lecithin, a natural emulsifier) and add flavour and colour to the finished ice cream. They help to prevent the formation of ice crystals, which is one argument for using eggs to eliminate (or at least reduce) the need for adding other stabilisers such as carob powder.

After a few years of experimenting when I was a pastry chef, I decided I preferred making gelato without eggs. That's not to say that there aren't some brilliant recipes that include them, but I love the purity of flavour you get from a simple dairy base (whether it be using milk/yoghurt/mascarpone/ricotta or cream). Not using eggs also means you do not have to make a custard, which is much less work and effort.

Crema rinforzata

Instead of eggs as the stabilisers in gelato, I use cornflour (cornstarch). *Crema rinforzata* as it's known, which means more-or-less 'reinforced custard', forms the base of many traditional Sicilian gelato recipes, and is a simple, pure-white mixture based on milk, sugar and cornflour, with the occasional addition of cream for richness and other flavouring. This milky gelato base has a 'clean' taste, which allows other flavours to truly shine, unsullied by the rich flavour of eggs. The cornflour works as an emulsifier and helps to prevent ice crystallisation, meaning that the desired chewy and smooth texture is easily achieved. This is an incredibly straightforward way of making gelato – economic too, using as it does only a few, very cheap everyday ingredients.

Fior di latte

The 'flower of the milk', this is the simplest and purest of all gelatos, made only from milk, sugar and a stabiliser (such as cornflour). The flavour is pure, sweet and simple, and this gelato is both used as a standard bearer for the quality of a gelateria and the base for many other flavours. It is often children's favourite flavour, and has the simple, clean, purity of a cold glass of milk (or the Mini Milks ice cream lollies I loved as a child in the UK).

Ricotta base

The second base I use to make gelato is the ricotta one on page 204. Equally pure, white and creamy, but with the characteristic richness of ricotta, this is a great base against which to balance sharp tangy fruit purées, or rich chocolate, coffee or nut flavours.

Mascarpone base

The final base gelato I use is a mascarpone one. It celebrates the velvety-creaminess of mascarpone and juxtaposes brilliantly with bright fruit flavours and fresh herbs such as mint.

Crème de la crème

A happy coincidence and echo of my past is the tradition of serving ice cream with extra cream – a dairy doubling that fills me with joy whenever I eat or encounter it.

Where I grew up in Devon it is common to serve ice cream with a scoop of clotted cream. The thick cream solidifies further to a beguilingly chewy texture, the flavour almost like butter, but sweeter, lighter, creamier. It is devilishly good. Gelato, too, is often eaten with whipped cream. Most often this combination is encountered in Sicily, but I've been offered *panna* (cream) with my gelato in Rome too (in the airport, no less!) and accepted it gleefully. Being so light and ethereal, it reinforces the flavour of whatever it's served with (the intensity of the chocolate in a chocolate gelato, for example) while the gentle creaminess also balances and cushions the intensity of that flavour. It's the perfect accompaniment. And, of course, gloriously decadent. Almost everything looks better with a soft blob of whipped cream on top of it (add a Maraschino cherry and I can die happy).

A sprinkling of history

As is also true of so many foodstuffs that have become pillars of Italian cuisine, the origins of gelato are hotly debated. There are the traditional Marco Polo and Catherine di Medici myths, both of which are spurned by many food historians. It is universally agreed, however, that the use of ice and the idea of flavouring it with liquids or fruits dates back to Roman times. Then, in the latter half of the 17th century, the creation of 'ices' spread across Europe. Recipes for ices began to be published in Naples and France about this time, and from then on the growth and diversification of ice cream as we now know it spread around the world. Gelato and the culture surrounding it (gelaterias, leisurely strolls with gelato in hand) is now inseparable with Italy, and one of the joys of Italian life.

Island delights

Sicily and Sardinia have cultivated a rich tradition of sweet-making, and also their own traditions when it comes to the invention and diversification of ices. Sicily's famous granitas, gelatos and sorbets have acquired a worldwide reputation and many of the distinctive flavours (jasmine, cinnamon, saffron, almond) have echoes of Sicily's Arabic occupation. No one can say for sure who invented ice cream, but the Sicilians have been famed makers for years, and it looks likely that they built upon the Arabic tradition of taking snow/ice and mixing it with fruit/sugar. Mary Taylor Simeti, in her book on Sicilian food *Pomp and Sustenance* writes:

'The Greeks and Romans employed lumps of Etna's snow to chill their wine, the Arabs used it instead to chill their *sarbat*. The Italian word *sorbetto* and the English sherbert come from these sweet fruit syrups that the Arabs drank diluted with ice water. The passage… to *granita* was only a question of time.'

Here in Sardinia there is a tradition of making a simple sorbet/ice known as *Sa Carapigna*. Developed in the 17th century, it is sold at fairs and festivals all over the island, and is produced according to ancient methods by one family. Born in the mountainous interior region of Aritzo, it grew out of the snow trade of the 17th century. In this region, winter snow was stored in wells, insulated by ferns, straw and earth, and then transported and sold throughout the year in the form of large blocks of ice. *Sa Carapigna* is still made according to the traditional recipe, using antique tools; a simple preparation of lemon, sugar and water is placed in a steel container, which in turn is placed inside a wooden barrel. The barrel is filled with large ice blocks and salt and the liquid rapidly stirred and turned until it freezes. I have tasted this simple sorbet at *sagre* (local food festivals) and it is deliciously refreshing.

MAKING GELATO AND ICE CREAM WITHOUT A MACHINE

I thought long and hard about the inclusion of gelato recipes in this book, as there can surely be nothing more disheartening than reading the instruction, 'buy an ice cream machine' if you do not have the space or budget. It is possible to make ice cream/gelato without an ice cream machine, but it is a bit more work. For the extreme satisfaction of creating your own flavour combinations I would say it was worth making, with or without a machine.

If you do not have an ice cream machine but you really want to make ice cream, don't worry, you still can! The ice creams made with cornflour (cornstarch) (such as the Chocolate Fudge Ice Cream on page 180 and the Rosemary *Fior di Latte* on page 208) can be frozen and scooped straight from the tub, as they are naturally chewy in texture.

Other recipes will need to be stirred/whisked/blitzed during the freezing process to prevent ice crystals forming.

To make ice cream this way:

- Pour your mix into a shallow container and cover with baking parchment. Place in the freezer.
- After 90 minutes, whisk (with a hand whisk) or blitz (in a blender or food processor) the mixture and then return it to the container and freezer.
- Repeat the process at least twice at intervals of 90 minutes.

Notes on storing ice cream

When storing ice creams/sorbets or granitas it is important to cover them closely and completely with baking parchment touching the surface, as well as a lid. This helps prevent random, unwanted ice crystals forming and also means they do not absorb the flavour of the air/freezer.

Sorbets and granitas (water ices)

Sorbets and granitas are traditionally made without cream or milk, and are usually based around fruits, herbs or flavoured syrups. Granita, however, is not churned but mashed/hashed up with a fork to create even frozen granules, or a sort of refined icy slush. Sorbets are traditionally churned and are thus smoother, airier and scoop-able. Both rely on a simple sugar syrup as their base, to which is added fruit or flavourings of your choice.

Lemon juice is essential for me in all water ices, to counteract the sweetness of the integral sugar syrup and highlight the flavour of the fruit. Good fruit makes good sorbets and good granitas, too. If you do not have an ice cream machine you can make any of the sorbet recipes in this book as a granita instead; they will work just as well.

Homemade granita can be a luxurious and lovely thing. Herbs make lovely granitas, mixed with a simple apple juice and lemon base (try tarragon or basil). Earl Grey teabags add a lovely aromatic note to a lemon- or peach-based granita. Rose petals and rose geranium leaves add a floral lift to berry fruit flavours. Thinking of drink combinations is a good place to start – gin and tonic granita, Campari and orange, peach and prosecco; the possibilities are endless.

The granita method

Once you have made your liquid base, decant it into a shallow container, put it in the freezer and leave for 1 hour.

Remove the container and mash up the contents evenly with a fork. Repeat this 3–4 more times at roughly 30-minute intervals until you have an even slush. Serve piled haphazardly in glasses.

Interestingly, if you want to turn a granita into a sorbet, you can simply throw it from the freezer into a high-strength blender, whizz it, and it will become a smooth sorbet ready to serve *subito*. I often do this with the coffee granita if I've had enough of eating it as granita and fancy a textural change. Icy alchemy!

Coffee & Brown Sugar Granita with Whipped Cream

Every morning I make a Moka coffee pot for six people and drink my way through half of it before the anxiety hits and my heart rate soars. At that point I think it's probably a good idea to stop drinking it – but it seems a cruel waste to throw it away, so instead I save it in a pot in the fridge and use it later for making this granita, or *Tiramisù*, or any other coffee-themed pudding.

I add a little Amaretto to the whipped cream because I love that retro almond whiff it gives, but you can leave it out. You can also top this with grated dark chocolate, or cocoa (unsweetened chocolate) powder, and serve with *Amaretti* (see p 34).

If you don't have a Moka pot (see p 38), you may have to ask your local barista nicely to make you a lot of espressos to take away.

Serves 6–8

500 ml (17 fl oz/2 cups) leftover strong espresso
5–6 tbsp light brown sugar
200 ml (7 fl oz/scant 1 cup) double (heavy) cream
1 tbsp icing (confectioner's) sugar
1 tbsp Amaretto

If the coffee is cold, warm it slightly so the sugar will dissolve easily. Stir in the sugar (add more to taste) until completely dissolved, then pour the mixture into a rectangular container, put in the freezer and leave for 1 hour.

After 1 hour, remove the container and mash the contents evenly with a fork. Repeat this 3–4 more times at roughly 30-minute intervals until you have an even, flaky slush.

Whip the cream, icing sugar and Amaretto to soft peaks in a mixing bowl.

Serve the granita and cream together in glasses.

Chocolate Fudge Ice Cream with Mascarpone

I'm not usually a great chocolate fan, but this ice cream is something really quite special. It's like the perfect (and rare) chocolate mousse you stumble upon and never forget, like the chocolate fudge pudding of your dreams. It also has a wonderfully chewy texture that accentuates this fudginess. It is intensely chocolatey, so I like to offset it with a big blob of mascarpone on top and sometimes some fresh orange zest too. If you want to make it fancy, you can add some (home!)-candied orange pieces.

It is also very good on its own.

Makes 1 litre (34 fl oz/4 cups)

720 ml (24 fl oz/3 cups) whole milk
50 g (2 oz/½ cup) cocoa (unsweetened chocolate) powder
200 g (7oz/¾ cup plus 2 tbsp) sugar
40 g (1½ oz/⅓ cup) cornflour (cornstarch)
70 g (2½ oz) dark chocolate, broken into pieces
1 tsp salt

To serve

mascarpone
orange zest or candied orange (see p 230) or Nut Brittle (see p 235)

Bring the milk and cocoa powder to a simmer in a saucepan, whisking continuously, and simmer for 5 minutes. Add the sugar and continue whisking over the heat.

Put the cornflour in a heatproof bowl and add a ladleful of the hot chocolate liquid. Whisk well until smooth. Pour and scrape this gooey mixture back into the warm chocolate mixture in the pan and cook for another few minutes, whisking all the time, as the mixture begins to thicken up like a custard.

Add the chocolate pieces and salt, and stir to melt. You should now have a thick, dark chocolate mixture.

Strain the mixture into a jug, allow it to cool and then pour into your ice-cream machine and churn according to the manufacturer's instructions. (Or to make by hand, see p 176.)

Serve with mascarpone and orange zest or candied orange. It also tastes delicious with a shard of nut brittle.

Green Lemon, Honey & Yoghurt Sorbet with Olive Oil

Frozen yoghurt sorbet, lifted by plenty of lemon and sweetened with honey, can be a lovely, light-but-creamy, tangy and refreshing thing to eat. It is delicious served with a punchy olive oil, the pepperiness cutting through the fat of the yoghurt perfectly. This is a celebration of four of my favourite ingredients: yoghurt, honey, lemon and olive oil.

In Sardinia, green lemons last all through the summer and into early autumn. They have a wonderful fresh, unripe flavour, much like a lime. If you want to replicate the flavour of green lemons, use two normal lemons and one lime.

Serves 6–8

zest and juice of 3 green lemons (or two lemons and one lime)
180 g (6 oz/¾ cup, plus 1 tbsp) sugar
30 ml (2 tbsp) water
500 ml (17fl oz) good Greek yoghurt
30 g (1 oz) honey

To serve

sea salt flakes
good olive oil

Finely zest the lemons or limes and put the zest, sugar and water in a small saucepan. Warm gently over a low heat and allow the sugar to melt (swirl the pan to speed up this process).

Simmer for a minute or two until you have a clear syrup.

Add the yoghurt, honey and citrus juice to the syrup and whisk well until smooth. Strain through a sieve, transfer to an ice-cream machine and churn according to the manufacturer's instructions. (Or to make by hand, see p 176.)

Serve with a sprinkling of sea salt flakes and a drizzle of your best punchy olive oil.

Note

Because of its higher water content, frozen yoghurt tends to go quite hard when frozen, so this is best eaten freshly churned, or re-churned before serving. Alternatively, allow to soften for a good 20 minutes in the fridge first.

128
SAMMONTANA
GELATI ALL'ITALIANA
SAMMONTANA
GELATI ALL'ITALIANA

Sparkling Lemon *Sorbetto* in Lemons

Lemon *sorbetto*, or simply *sorbetto* as it is known here in Sardinia, is an example of one of the purest and simplest of sorbets (originally made from just three ingredients: water, sugar and lemon) that has become mass-produced.

Most bars and *trattorias* will have a large plastic machine constantly churning a slushy white lemon *sorbetto* mix to be sold in little champagne flutes with a straw at the end of a meal. It has a fizziness and freshness (like a sherbert), I wanted to replicate in my own kitchen. It is the most refreshing thing in the world, and I am convinced that the slight saltiness of a natural sparkling water enhances the zing. Serve in the hollowed-out lemon shells for added effect.

Makes 1 litre (34 fl oz/4 cups), enough to fill around 6 lemons

250 ml (8½ fl oz/1 cup) lemon juice (roughly the juice of 8 small lemons), plus the zest of 1 lemon
280 g (10 oz/1¼ cups) sugar
100 ml (3½ fl oz/scant ½ cup) water
200 ml (7 fl oz/scant 1 cup) fizzy water (use a salty brand like San Pellegrino)

If you wish to serve this inside the lemons, cut off 1 cm (½ in) from the bottom of the fruits to create a flat surface for them to stand upright. Cut the top off (a larger 2–3 cm (¾–1¼ in) here to create a good hat) and reserve as a lid. Scoop out all of the flesh as if preparing a Halloween pumpkin and squeeze the flesh through a sieve to obtain the juice for your *sorbetto*. Freeze the lemon shells before using them to serve the sorbet; they look much more effective slightly frosty, and will keep the *sorbetto* colder for longer.

Finely grate the zest from one of the lemons and put this in a small saucepan.

Add the sugar and the still water to the saucepan and bring to the boil. Simmer for 3–5 minutes until syrupy.

Strain the syrup through a sieve into a bowl (discard the zest). Stir in the lemon juice and the fizzy water.

Transfer to an ice-cream machine and churn according to the manufacturer's instructions. (Or to make by hand, see p 176.)

Serve in the hollowed-out lemons.

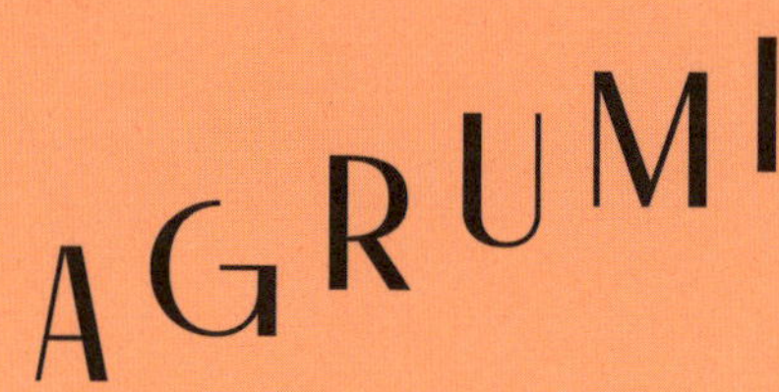

Citrus

The day I arrived in Sardinia I stepped out of the tiny, empty train station in Oristano and was greeted by a cluster of orange trees. Beneath them lay a few large, dimpled oranges, their skins baggy and split, their pale insides spilling onto the ground. Here I was in a place where citrus fruit was so bountiful it fell off the tree and was left to rot.

My love affair with citrus, however, had begun long before this.

Every holiday of my childhood, when we travelled to sunnier climes, my mother would routinely screech at my dad to stop the car at the sight of a citrus tree overhanging the road, or some waxy orange or yellow windfalls on the verge. She couldn't resist their inflated size, their intoxicating scent, their uneven shape; so different to those round, small, smooth and scentless beasts we found in Tesco at home.

We would travel home with mum's case stuffed half-full of stolen citrus, and she would make us a prawn cocktail (frozen prawns, naturally) with a special, smuggled wedge of huge and juicy holiday lemon as a treat. Oranges at home were for Christingle, or came ready juiced in cartons of Tropicana. Clementines were just for Christmas and were always dry and overly sweet. As long as I have known her, my mother has worshipped and craved citrus, and always tried in vain to grow her own lemons. She is on roughly her fifteenth sapling now, and occasionally one of them will produce a small and sad fruit, which she sends me triumphant photos of.

Though citrus may well seem innately and indisputably Mediterranean, citrus fruits were first cultivated in China or India around 2200 BCE, and most probably only travelled into Italy via Sicily with the Arabs in the 10th century, along with so many things that now form the pillars of the Mediterranean diet.

Initially grown ornamentally and used for perfumes rather than consumed, the first oranges were inedible and bitter, like those first trees I spied when I arrived in Sardinia. The orange takes its name from the Dravidian Indian word, *narayam* meaning 'perfume within', which eventually became the Italian word *arancia*. Another wonderful word associated with citrus is *zagara*, which is the Sicilian word for the blossom. It derives from *zahara*, an Arabic word meaning 'splendour' or 'sparkling white'. From 'sparkling white' to 'perfume within' – even the language associated with citrus is romantic and evocative.

Aromatherapy

It is not only me and my mother who find ourselves lifted, elated even, by lemons; citrus fruit of all varieties has enticed and bewitched people throughout the centuries. Living next to a lemon tree, as I happily do, provides year-round pleasure and three separate sources of joy: the glossy evergreen leaves, the glowing fruit and the star-shaped, highly perfumed blossom, which at certain points of the year, exists in conjunction with the fruit. The sight of real lemons and oranges growing on real trees is one that I will never tire of, and even after nearly four years in Italy I pause in public parks and on street corners to photograph citrus trees.

Of course, an orange is really a simple thing, now so commonplace to almost all of us, available as they are all year round from all corners of the world. But considering it anew, plucked from its glossy canopy of deep green leaves rather than from a shelf in a shop, it is truly worthy of the rapture and wonder felt by every visitor to the Mediterranean from colder and less citrus-blessed climes. Its globe-like shape, its weight in the hand, the multiple tiny dimples, and the aroma released when you scratch the skin inspire an immediate sigh of pleasure. An orange's very architecture is pleasing too: an inherently generous fruit, designed to be shared, with each juicy segment perfectly contained within its own papery white case.

Citrus has long been recognised for its curative properties, both physical and mental. Unlike many mammals, we humans do not produce our own Vitamin C, so we must ingest it. Scurvy, or *scorbuto* as it is known in Italian, is a disease caused by lack of Vitamin C, and *scorbutico* is an adjective I hear often in everyday parlance in Sardinia. It means cantankerous, or grumpy, and the connection to a lack of the therapeutic properties provided by citrus is deeply pleasing to someone like me, who sees the world and all its elements through an edible lens.

Equally, citrus is often claimed to have antidepressant qualities, particularly the essential oils from the *Citrus bergamia*. During the bleak winter months I frequently burn bergamot oil in an oil burner, and there can be no denying that during the darkest winter days, the sight of a bowl of bright clementines and their waxy green leaves is infinitely cheering.

Citrus in the kitchen

The joy of citrus fruit in the kitchen is twofold: the sharp juice and the aromatic zest, both of which are invaluable. In some cases, such as with *cedro* (citron), a large citrus fruit with a thick pith, the joy is threefold as the pith is eaten too – as is the case with some of the best lemons, which can be sliced thinly and eaten with oil and salt as a sort of salad.

There are very few sweet or savoury dishes that are not improved by the addition of citrus. A rich cake batter or ricotta filling is lifted by lemon zest, and a spritz of the juice brings out the best in almost all fruit. When making granitas and sorbets, the acidity and freshness lemon juice provides is invaluable.

When choosing oranges and lemons, I am always drawn to the ugliest. Looks are not everything, and the least aesthetically blessed tend to be the most juicy and aromatic. The more knobbly and deeply dimpled it is, the better – ideally untreated, unwaxed, and with the leaf still attached. Though the leaf may not be edible it gives me great pleasure, and is at least proof that the lemon was picked fairly recently.

Monstrous fruit

One of the most extraordinary (and rare) citrus fruits I have come across in Italy is the *Pompia*. *Sa Pompia,* as it is known in Sardo, is a citrus fruit native to Sardinia and found only in specific regions. It is thought to be one of the rarest citrus fruits in the world. Its botanic name, *Citrus monstrouso*, hints at its so-called ugly appearance. It is large, round and squat, as pockmarked as a witch's nose, and is thought to be a hybrid of a lemon and a *cedro*.

Here in Sardinia it is candied whole, very slowly in honey, to produce a wonderful, shining amber globe, which is eaten in sacred slices. The flavour is extraordinarily floral and delicate, retaining all of the fruit's aromatic qualities (those of zest, juice and pith) and none of its original bitterness.

Mascarpone Ice Cream

This is a perfect, creamy base gelato onto which you can build as you see fit, allowing you to create any flavour you can think of. The intense creaminess of the mascarpone is lightly offset by the tangy yoghurt. It's the perfect gelato to use for making a fruit ripple flavour; cook whichever fruit is good or in season, and ripple it through as it churns. Or, make a simple fruit purée (by poaching and then puréeing it, as on p 194) and whisk it into this base before churning.

Makes 1 litre (34 fl oz/4 cups)

220 g (8 oz/1 cup) sugar
100 ml (3½ fl oz/scant ½ cup) water
pinch of salt
400 g (14 oz) mascarpone
100 g (3½ oz) Greek yoghurt
250 ml (8½ fl oz/1 cup) milk

First make a sugar syrup: put the sugar, water and pinch of salt in a small saucepan and bring to the boil, swirling the pan to help dissolve the sugar. Simmer over a low heat for about 3 minutes, until the syrup is shiny and just slightly thicker.

Allow to cool for a minute.

In a large bowl, whisk the mascarpone, yoghurt and milk together to form a smooth creamy mixture. Once the syrup has cooled slightly, whisk it into this mixture. (If the sugar syrup seizes up at this point and turns hard, place the whole lot over a low heat again, whisking until you have a smooth mixture.)

Transfer to an ice-cream machine and churn according to the manufacturer's instructions. (Or to make by hand, see p 176.) Store in an airtight container.

Other possibilities

Infuse the milk with a handful of roasted coffee beans to make a simple coffee/mascarpone gelato, or do the same with a cup of well-roasted almonds.

Mascarpone & Fresh Mint Choc Chip

One of the saddest things about living in Italy has been the discovery that mint choc chip does not really exist in the majority of *gelaterie*. Mint choc chip is – perhaps unsurprisingly – an English invention, created in the 70s by a culinary student as part of a competition for Princess Anne's wedding. Originally – and rather grandly – named 'Mint Royale' it became an instant hit, and is now one of the world's most popular ice cream flavours. I am not ashamed to admit I still feel a tug on my heart strings every time I see the lurid peppermint green version, heavily dyed with food colouring and full of false flavouring.

Makes 1 litre (34 fl oz/4 cups)

1 batch of Mascarpone Ice Cream (see left)
20 g (¾ oz) mint leaves
60 g (2 oz) dark chocolate, melted in a bain marie (see p 255)

Pluck the mint leaves from their stalks and wash them, then pat them dry between pieces of kitchen paper.

Place the mint leaves in a bowl with the mascarpone mixture and using a stick blender blend the whole mixture well until the mint is only visible in very tiny flecks.

If you wish to strain it at this point, then you can do so. I leave the flecks of mint in.

Churn the ice cream mixture in your ice cream machine then when it has just reached soft set, after 40 minutes or so. (Or to make by hand, see p 176.)

To make the *Stracciatella*, smooth out a third of your frozen gelato into a plastic container. Using a spoon zig zag a small amount of the melted chocolate back and forth over the surface. Spoon over the second third of the gelato and repeat the zig zagging. Do this one final time then, using a spoon, stir the gelato to evenly distribute the chocolate.

Blackberry Mascarpone Ripple Ice Cream

Stir this blackberry purée through the Mascarpone Ice Cream (see p 192) after churning for a ripple effect. Alternatively you can stir the purée into the mixture before churning for an evenly purple ice cream.

Makes 1 litre (34 fl oz/4 cups)

1 x batch of Mascarpone Ice Cream base (see p 192)
260 g (9½ oz) blackberries
zest and juice of 1 lemon
1 tbsp sugar
1 tbsp water

First make the ice-cream base according to the instructions on page 192.

Put the blackberries, lemon zest, sugar and water in a saucepan and cook over a low heat, covered with a lid, until the fruit is soft. Add the lemon juice and then, using a stick blender, blitz to form a purée.

Churn the ice cream mixture in your ice-cream machine, according to the manufacturer's directions, then when it has just reached soft set, after 40 minutes or so, scoop it out into an airtight plastic container. (Or to make by hand, see p 176.)

While it's still soft, ripple through the blackberry purée. Freeze in an airtight container.

Peach & Basil Sorbet

I always want to be a sorbet sort of person, but inevitably I fall (willingly) down the pistachio gelato rabbit-hole, and I almost never order gelato's frostier and fruitier *sorbetto* sister. The problem with sorbet is that I find it can be a little bit too light. Most of the time I feel the need for something a bit denser. That is why this sorbet is so wonderful, because the velvety peach purée that it produces has substantial body, and doesn't really feel flimsily light at all; instead silky, thick and luxurious.

The last week or two of July, when the days are peach-sticky with heat, is when I will finally want sorbet. The peaches at this time are like the peaches of your wildest dreams, the 'Giant Peaches' of Roald Dahl's *James*. Fleshy and drunk with juice and sweetness, their downy jackets paper-thin, puncturing under a careless nail when held in a hot hand.

I love using herbs and basil is the archetypal herb of high summer. I have paired it before in a peach jam, and I eat it in one of my favourite summer salads: prosciutto, basil and peaches (sometimes I add burrata for gentle overkill). The combination is so good I thought it would make a good sorbet (minus the prosciutto). So here it is; maybe once you've tried it, you too will eschew precious pistachio at last.

If you want to replace the basil with mint, it also works very well.

Makes 1 litre (34 fl oz/4 cups)

200 g (7 oz/¾ cup, plus 2 tbsp) sugar
100 ml (3½ fl oz/scant ½ cup) water
20 leaves of fresh basil, washed, patted dry and torn (one bunch should easily supply this many)
750 g (1 lb 10 oz) very ripe peaches
zest and juice of 2 lemons

Bring the sugar and water to the boil in a small saucepan. Allow to simmer for 1 minute (swirl the pan to make sure the sugar has melted but do not stir). Once you have a clear, shiny, thick syrup, remove from the heat. Drop in the basil leaves, then decant the syrup into a glass jug or bowl to cool. Cover.

Cut the peaches into chunks and macerate them with the lemon zest and the lemon juice. (I just peel this in strips with a swivel-peeler here as everything will be blitzed and strained eventually but you can finely zest it if you prefer.)

When the syrup has cooled, pour it over the peaches and leave the whole lot to infuse for a few hours at room temperature (or covered in the fridge overnight).

Blend everything (leaves, zest and peach flesh) in a blender until you have a smooth purée.

Sieve the mixture, discarding the bits of basil left behind in the sieve, making sure to press the pulp to extract all the flavours and juices.

Transfer to an ice-cream machine and churn according to the manufacturer's instructions. (Or to make by hand, see p 176.)

Store in an airtight container.

Pear, Lemon & Lemon Verbena Sorbet

At the tail end of summer tiny little pears with the slightest pink blush and waxy yellow skin appear at the market. To a foreign eye like mine, used to fat-bellied Conference pears, they initially look hard, small and under-ripe. They are, in fact, some of the sweetest and juiciest I have ever tasted, and are called Coscia pears – edible proof that appearances can be misleading.

At the same time of year, lemon verbena, or *Maria Luisa* as it's known in Italian, is in full swing, and has a wonderful scent and flavour that marries particularly well with pear. This is such a lovely light, fresh and fragrant combination, the flavour of a crisp September morning, and the flavours match so well it makes you wonder where the pear ends and the verbena begins. If you can find Coscia pears I recommend them. If not, another good flavourful variety will do fine.

Makes 1 litre (34 fl oz/4 cups)

150 g (5 oz/⅔ cup) sugar
280 ml (9½ fl oz/1 cup, plus 2 tbsp) water
6–7 good ripe pears (around 800 g/1 lb 12 oz), ideally Coscia
juice of 2 large lemons
8–9 fresh lemon verbena leaves

Make a simple sugar syrup by bringing the sugar and water to a gentle simmer in a small saucepan. Allow to simmer (swirl the pan to make sure the sugar has melted but do not stir) for 1 minute. Once you have a clear, shiny, thick syrup, remove from the heat.

Peel and core the pears, cutting them into rough pieces (if they begin to brown, introduce some lemon juice to the proceedings, but if you work swiftly it should be fine). Drop them immediately in the syrup and cover with a piece of baking parchment (this prevents them from discolouring). Leave to poach for 2–3 minutes. Remove from the heat and add half of the lemon verbena leaves. Leave the whole lot to infuse for 10–20 minutes.

Remove the lemon verbena leaves and discard them. In a blender or food processor, blend the pears and their syrup along with the lemon juice and the fresh verbena leaves until you have a pulp.

Strain through a fine sieve (discard the solids left behind in the sieve), transfer to an ice-cream machine and churn according to the manufacturer's instructions. (Or to make by hand, see p 176; or you can freeze the mixture as for granita, see p 177.)

Store in an airtight container.

Ricotta & Fig Ripple Gelato

There is something about a ripple that is magical. Even the word itself is wonderful. Raspberry ripple was my favourite ice cream flavour as a child; the vivid scarlet swirls shining through the sundae glass in acute contrast to the primrose yellow of the vanilla. Ricotta and fig is a gelato flavour I have seen and tasted in *gelaterie* across Italy but can be disappointing, so I decided to make my own. You will need extra-ripe and jammy figs for this.

Makes 1 litre (34 fl oz/4 cups)

For the ricotta gelato base

400 ml (13 fl oz/generous 1½ cups) milk
140 g (4½ oz/⅔ cup) sugar
15 g (½ oz) cornflour (cornstarch)
250 g (9 oz) ricotta
pinch of sea salt

For the fig purée

280 g (10 oz) extremely ripe figs, washed and de-stemmed
1 tbsp mild honey
juice of ½ a small lemon (1 tbsp)

For the gelato base, bring the milk and sugar to a simmer in a saucepan, stirring occasionally to help melt the sugar.

Put the cornflour in a bowl and add a ladleful of the hot milk mixture to it, whisking well to form a smooth paste. Return the cornflour mixture to the pan with the milk and whisk well over a low heat for a few minutes until the mixture becomes the consistency of a thin custard or double (heavy) cream.

Remove from the heat and allow to cool for a few minutes.

Meanwhile, make the fig purée by blending all the ingredients together until smooth. (If your figs are less ripe, see note below.)

Once the base mixture has slightly cooled, add the ricotta mixture and salt. In a blender or using a stick blender, blitz the mixture well. Strain through a sieve (discard the solids left in the sieve), transfer to an ice-cream machine and churn according to manufacturer's instructions. (Or to make by hand, see p 176.) Once frozen but still soft, stir through the fig purée gently with a spoon to create a pale green ripple. Store in an airtight container.

Other ricotta ripple possibilities

You can make other fruit purées and ripple them through the ricotta base in place of the fig purée above. Other flavours that work well are:

- Apricot purée
- Peach and basil purée (see Peach & Basil Sorbet, p 198)
- Blackberry purée (see Blackberry Mascarpone Ripple Ice Cream, p 194)
- Simply ripple through a honey of your choice

Note

Ideally you will have extremely ripe figs, and you can purée them directly with the lemon and honey. Green figs are best (known as white figs in Italy). If they are less ripe, poach them in a small pan with 2 tablespoons water and 2 tablespoons of sugar with a lid on, on a very gentle heat, until they are collapsing and soft enough to purée. Drain off any remaining liquid and purée them with the lemon and honey to get a good figgy consistency.

Ricotta, Honey & Coffee Gelato

One of my favourite breakfasts is a lily-white slab of fresh ricotta drizzled with good honey and a black coffee. This gelato is a celebration of that delicious combination. The smoky bitter notes of the coffee are underlined by a golden, woody depth from the honey, and the ricotta unites and mellows the two, wrapping them in an unapologetic blanket of creaminess.

Makes just under 1 litre (34 fl oz/4 cups)

400 ml (13 fl oz/generous 1½ cups) milk
120 g (4 oz/½ cup) caster (superfine) sugar
10 g (4 tsp) cornflour (cornstarch)
250 g (9 oz) ricotta
pinch of salt
1 tbsp coffee grounds
1 tbsp good flavourful honey, to drizzle

Bring the milk and sugar to a simmer in a saucepan, stirring occasionally to help melt the sugar.

Put the cornflour in a bowl and add a ladleful of the hot milk mixture to it, whisking well to form a smooth paste. Return the cornflour mixture to the pan with the milk and whisk well over a low heat for a few minutes until the mixture becomes the consistency of double (heavy) cream.

Remove from the heat and allow to cool for a few minutes.

Once slightly cooled, add the ricotta and the salt and blitz the mixture well, either in the pan using a stick blender or in a blender. Strain through a fine sieve into a bowl (discard the solids left in the sieve) and add the coffee grounds. Transfer to an ice-cream machine and churn according to the manufacturer's instructions. (Or to make by hand, see p 176.)

Serve with the honey drizzled over the top.

Note

If you prefer, you can stir the honey through the mixture with the coffee grounds, rather than serving it on top.

Gelato

Rosemary *Fior di Latte*

The ultimate test of a good *gelateria* is their *Fior di Latte* gelato. Containing no additional flavours, it should provide the perfect demonstration of the quality of the milk/cream mixture they use. Meaning 'flower of the milk', the simple, unadorned gelato is the equivalent of an icy-cold glass of milk on a hot day – pure, unadulterated, and a celebration of cool, lactic sweetness. It is the favourite of many children, and has a white purity that is irresistible.

The addition of rosemary makes this slightly more adult and especially delicious. Rosemary has an oily pungency reminiscent of both lemon peel and pine needles which works so well with sweet or creamy flavours, and also with all citrus. This is based on a recipe by the brilliant food writer and cook, Emiko Davies.

Makes 1 litre (34 fl oz/4 cups)

700 ml (24 fl oz/scant 3 cups) milk
200 ml (7 fl oz/scant 1 cup) cream
200 g (7 oz/¾ cups, plus 2 tbsp) sugar
25 g (1 oz/3½ tbsp) cornflour (cornstarch)
1 sprig of fresh rosemary, washed
pinch of salt

Bring the milk, cream and sugar to a simmer in a saucepan.

Put the cornflour in a heatproof bowl, add a ladleful of the hot milk liquid, and whisk well until completely smooth. Return this mixture to the saucepan and continue to cook over a low heat, whisking continuously, until the mixture thickens to a custard consistency. Add the rosemary and salt and remove from the heat.

Leave to infuse for at least 10 minutes, then sieve into a bowl or jug, pressing well to extract all the flavour of the rosemary (discard the solids left in the sieve). Transfer the mixture to an ice-cream machine and churn according to the manufacturer's instructions. (Or to make by hand, see p 176.)

Store in an airtight container.

Note

This is also very good served with pine nut brittle. Or with fresh figs. Or with a drizzle of *sapa* (see p 14) or *abbamele* (see p 245). The possibilities are endless.

Strawberry & Whole Lemon *Sorbetto*

Sadly, this life is full of disappointing strawberries. I have a Sardinian friend here who once said, with such solemnity it was almost comical, 'There is nothing worse in life than a bad strawberry.' Nothing worse!

This sorbet, however, tastes how you always wish strawberries would taste. The lemon acts as an enhancer, bringing out the best in the fruit as it does in everything. It's an unusual recipe in that the lemon is blitzed up – pith and all – so you get the truest lemon flavour – the pungent, aromatic oils from the skin and the fresh acidity from the juice and flesh. This makes the sorbet enormously refreshing and almost sherbert-like, thanks to the fizz of the citrus. The lemon is extra important here (see notes on citrus on p 188). Of course, it still makes a difference to use the very best strawberries you can find.

Makes 1 litre (34 fl oz/4 cups)

700 g (1 lb 9 oz) strawberries
½ large lemon
pinch of sea salt
200 g (7 oz/¾ cups, plus 2 tbsp) sugar
50 ml (3 tbsp) water

Hull the strawberries carefully, rinse them briefly in cold water and put them in a bowl.

Remove any pips from your lemon half then chop it into rough chunks and mix it with the strawberries. Add the sea salt.

Make a simple sugar syrup by heating the sugar and water in a small pan over a low heat. Swirl gently to dissolve the sugar and allow to simmer for a minute or so, until you have a clear, gel-like syrup. Pour the syrup over the chopped lemons and strawberries, transfer to a food processor and blitz the whole lot until you have a smooth purée.

Sieve the mixture into a jug or bowl to remove any pieces of pith (discard). Transfer to an ice-cream maker and churn according to the manufacturer's instructions (Or to make by hand, see p 176; or you can freeze the mixture as for granita, see p 177.) Store in an airtight container.

PUFFO

Life, love, people, places, food: all are full of contradictions. Italy, like most places in the world, has these in spades.

Puffo provides an important lesson in not becoming overly romantic about Italian food, a trap almost all of us starry-eyed *stranieri* fall into, and for this reason, I love it wholeheartedly. True love, after all, is the recognition and acceptance of imperfection, and I love Italian food almost as much for its imperfections as its perfections.

Puffo is a gelato found in a large proportion of *gelaterie* all over Italy. Named after the Smurfs (Puffo is the generic name for Smurf), Puffo was invented in the 1980s to honour the enormously popular TV show of the same name. I knew of the Smurfs growing up in the UK, but I was delighted to discover their evocatively named Italian relatives, and even more delighted to discover their eponymous gelato.

Puffo is bluer than the bluest blue; tantalisingly, terrifyingly, toothpaste blue, and is not really a flavour at all. Instead it is just a simple *fior di latte* base, dyed blue with colouring. Occasionally – depending on the place – it is bubble-gum flavoured. It is principally designed for children, though there is nothing to stop adults ordering a scoop if they want to.

There are very few blue foods in the world, possibly for good reason, but I can't help feeling extremely fond of Puffo, not only for the bright blue wake-up call it gives me every time I am in danger of becoming too misty-eyed about Italian food culture, but also because it provides me with the happy, nostalgic memory of the blue Mr Freeze lollies I adored when I was a child.

Beware the Puffo ...

Regardless of my nostalgic fondness for Puffo, it must be said that it serves another purpose: it is often the sign of a so-called 'bad' *gelateria*. I hesitate to fundamentally categorise *gelaterie* into good or bad, as life is rarely so simple, but let's just say that the gelato in Puffo-inclusive *gelaterie* is often likely to be filled with artificial additives and flavourings.

The more colourful a gelato display is, the more elaborate the toppings that crown its cascades of fluorescent gelato, the more fake the product is likely to be. The purists say that true gelato, the high-quality, made-from-scratch-with-good-ingredients type, must be kept in chilled, cylindrical stainless-steel containers with lids (this way, the temperature is totally controlled) so that you can't see it at all until it is scooped out for you. When it comes to decoration, sometimes less is more.

Natural colours: the deep-purple, wine colour of a good berry sorbet, or the murky pond-green of a true pistachio, are good indicators of quality. Few flavours and a focus on seasonal varieties also suggest quality. Paddles rather than scoops indicate real, soft, scoopable gelato, as does a matte (rather than shiny) texture. Anything to do with Kinder or cookies is contentious.

While Italy prides itself on the authenticity and quality of its food culture, it is not immune to Puffi, or to industrialised production, and really good-quality *gelaterie* are relatively few and far between. I like (almost) all gelato, whether truly high quality or not, but when you find the real thing it is a wonderful experience, as is making your own at home.

Just beware the Smurf.

7

GIFTS

One of the greatest things about cooking is making edible things to give to people as gifts. Every Christmas, birthday, Easter or other festivity provides the opportunity to create something delicious to give to the people you love. Creating edible gifts is satisfying on many levels: it's usually cheaper than buying them, it shows that you've gone to a lot more effort than just clicking a button on Amazon, and theoretically (and perhaps selfishly), it should be a fun activity for you too.

My granny (she of the bedside biscuits) was a great believer in both giving gifts and buying/making gifts for herself. She used to address a little something wrapped up with a card

'From my darling little self
to my darling little self.'

I am also a big believer in buying (and making) all manner of gifts, many of which may never actually make the journey outside my own home. But then again, many of them do. Gifting, whether to yourself or others, is always satisfying.

I used to make and give the same granny homemade jars of chutney and jam every year, only for her to re-gift them to me the following one, saying, 'I'm not sure WHO gave me this, but I think you should have it. I don't know what *I'll* do with it!' Failing re-gifting them to me, she would take them to other people's houses when she was invited for lunch.

Whether we pass them on or not, we all love giving gifts, and we also all love receiving them; so we can continue this strange and beautiful cycle and have a go at making some of the following recipes.

Little Soft-Hearted Lemon & Almond Meringues

Bianchini, 'little white ones', or *Bianchittus* in Sardo, are small meringues popular in Sardinia and offered as *dolci*. They are often eaten as is, with nothing added, and they are astonishingly delicious. The secret is to add lemon zest and toasted nibbed almonds. This way, they are lighter, zestier, nuttier, and they are always cooked just enough so that they are still chewy in the middle. I could eat a handful on their own, but they also work very well beside ice cream, or with coffee. After tasting these you'll never make a plain meringue again.

Traditionally, these little meringues were cooked in a wood-fired oven, after all the bread had been baked and there were just a few embers and a low enough temperature to cook them gently. There is a legend which states that whoever cooks them must be alone, so as not to be distracted from watching them constantly. Here in Sardinia they are prepared for special occasions and almost always decorated with multi coloured sprinkles or little silver balls.

This mixture of the two sugars makes for a smoother texture – icing (confectioner's) sugar means the finished meringue has a chalkier edge, while the caster sugar gives it shine and a crisp texture.

Makes 20 egg-size meringues

40 g (1½ oz) whole blanched almonds
140 g (5 oz/1 cup, plus 2 tbsp) icing (confectioner's) sugar
60 g (¼ cup) caster (superfine) sugar
finely grated zest of 1 lemon
100 g (3½ oz) egg whites (from 3 medium eggs)
multi-coloured sprinkles, to decorate

Preheat the oven to 170°C (340°F/Gas 3).

Nib the almonds (slice them lengthways into rough shards) and place them on a baking sheet. Toast in the oven for 8 minutes, or until just beginning to turn golden. Remove from the oven and leave to cool. Turn the oven down to 110°C (230°F/Gas ¼).

Measure out the two types of sugar and combine them in a mixing bowl.

Finely zest the lemon onto a piece of absorbent kitchen paper and pat the zest dry by folding the absorbent paper in half and pressing it gently (this will eliminate some liquid from the zest).

In a large clean mixing bowl and using an electric mixer, whisk the egg whites for 2–3 minutes until they are white and foamy. Add a spoonful of the sugar mixture and continue whisking at a high speed. Keep adding spoonful by spoonful of the sugar mixture and whisking well until you have a smooth, stiff, shiny meringue. It should be perfectly smooth and opaque, and stiff enough to hold its shape. Gently fold in the lemon zest.

Line 2 baking sheets with baking parchment. If spooning the mixture, you can fold the toasted almonds through now, then using

a dessert spoon, dollop the mixture onto the prepared baking sheet. If piping it, the almond nibs are too big to easily squeeze through the piping nozzle so sprinkle them on after you have piped the meringues. Size-wise you can decide; any size from strawberry up to peach-size is good.

Transfer the meringues to the oven. Bake for 1–1½ hours, depending on the size of the meringues.

To check if they are cooked sufficiently, as in cooked enough to hold their shape and be servable, remove the baking sheet from the oven, lift a meringue up and tap the bottom very gently. If it is crisp and dry, then the meringues are cooked sufficiently to serve. The longer you cook them, the more they will dry out, so that eventually you will eliminate all squidginess from the middle and end up with a crisp, completely dry meringue.

Decorate with multi-coloured sprinkles before serving.

These will keep in an airtight container for up to 2 months.

Capezzoli di Venere

I first heard about these 'Nipples of Venus' after watching the film *Amadeus*, when they are offered by the devious Salieri to Mrs Mozart, and their salacious beauty makes a second cinematic appearance in *Chocolat*. A white chocolate exterior is traditional to mimic the snow-white beauty of Venus' breast, but I choose to coat these in dark chocolate as I prefer the flavour, and they look even more striking with their pink nipples.

These make a beautiful gift, perfect for Valentine's Day, Christmas, Mother's Day, weddings – any occasion, really. I always make them for my mum, who has a great love of chestnuts.

The chestnuts give these a delicious smoky, woody edge, which is enhanced by the brandy. They are even better if made with *marron glacé*.

Makes 16

150 g (5 oz) dark chocolate (at least 70 per cent cocoa solids)
30 g (1 oz) butter
40 g (1½ oz/¼ cup) light brown sugar
140 ml (5 fl oz/scant ⅔ cup) double (heavy) cream
40 g (1½ oz) cooked chestnuts, chopped into small pieces, or *marron glacé*
a few drops of vanilla extract
a pinch of salt
10 ml (2 tsp) brandy (optional)

To coat

200 g (7 oz) dark chocolate (at least 70 per cent cocoa solids)

For the 'nipples'

50 g (2 oz) white chocolate chips
1–2 drops red food colouring

Chop the 150g (5 oz) chocolate into small pieces by hand or blitz in a blender and transfer to a heatproof bowl.

Put the butter, sugar and cream in a small saucepan and bring to a simmer.

Once simmering, pour the hot cream mixture over the chocolate and stir until the chocolate has melted. Add the chopped chestnuts, vanilla, salt and brandy (if using). Stir to combine.

Chill in the fridge until firm (2–3 hours). When firm take teaspoonfuls of the mixture and roll them into balls between your hands. Put on a baking sheet lined with baking parchment and chill again until solid (you can also put them in the freezer at this point to speed up the process).

Line a baking sheet with baking parchment.

For the coating, melt the dark chocolate in a heatproof bowl over a bain-marie (see p 255).

For the 'nipples', melt the white chocolate in a separate heatproof bowl (see p 255). Mix in a drop or two of the food colouring to create a light pink colour. Make a little piping bag out of a square of greaseproof (waxed) paper and spoon the pink chocolate into it (it will need to be kept warm so it doesn't solidify).

Using a fork, skewer the chilled truffles and dip them in the melted dark chocolate, making sure they are fully covered.

Place them on the prepared baking sheet. Pipe the pink nipples on top and then allow to set. Keep chilled and eat within 10 days.

Note

If you wish to use white chocolate to coat the truffles you can – just be aware that it never melts very well so it will be harder to coat the truffles evenly.

Chocolate, Hazelnut & Sour Cherry *Salame*

I used to always request chocolate biscuit cake (also known as fridge cake) as my birthday cake, which was a blow to my mum because she had a special talent for inventive cake decoration, and chocolate biscuit cake is almost impossible to decorate. Nevertheless, this combination of broken biscuits, chocolate and butter was my favourite cake as a child; strange on many counts, as generally I've never been a lover of chocolate, and it isn't *really* a cake.

Anyway, I loved it, and I still love it, and I also love its Italian cousin, which has the added bonus of being shaped like a *Salame*. This *Salame* can be wrapped and presented as a gift (perfect for Christmas/Easter/birthdays) or served in slices as a surprisingly sophisticated and simple pudding, with a coffee.

This recipe is infinitely adaptable. Dried cherries have an irresistible chewiness and slight sourness, which works very well here. For the most simple salami you can omit all nuts and dried fruit, keeping only the biscuits chunks, and it is still delicious. You can swap the cherries for dried figs (nice, crunchy seediness), cranberries, dates, prunes, apricots or even raisins. You can also add a splash of rum, Amaretto or any booze you choose. Pistachios can be added instead for a pop of lime-green colour, or almonds, or a mix of any nuts you fancy.

Makes 1 (almost obscenely) large *Salame*, or two modest *Salami*

80 g (3 oz) hazelnuts
200 g (7 oz) biscuits (Rich Tea or another simple, dry, not-too-sweet biscuit)
250 g (9 oz) dark chocolate (at least 70 per cent cocoa solids)
150 g (5 oz) butter (at room temperature)
120 g (4 oz/½ cup) caster (superfine) sugar
pinch of salt
2 eggs, beaten
1 tbsp cocoa (unsweetened chocolate) powder
80 g (3 oz) dried cherries (you can substitute cranberries or any other fruit you wish)
icing (confectioner's) sugar, for dusting

Preheat the oven to 170°C (340°F/Gas 3). Lay the hazelnuts over the base of a baking sheet. Toast them in the oven for 10 minutes or so until lightly golden. Remove and set aside to cool, then roughly chop (or crush them briefly with the bottom of a rolling pin).

Break up the biscuits by putting them in a bag and bashing them with a rolling pin or by blitzing them quickly in a food processor. It is important they stay in fairly large pieces – you're not aiming for crumbs.

Melt the chocolate in a small heatproof bowl set over a pan of gently simmering water (or in a microwave) (see p 255). Allow it to cool for a few minutes.

Beat the butter, sugar and salt in a mixing bowl using an electric mixer until smooth and creamy. Whisk in the beaten eggs, a little at a time, to form a smooth batter. Add the cocoa powder and the cooled, melted chocolate. Add the broken biscuits and the dried cherries and stir well to combine. Add the hazelnuts and stir again.

Scoop the mixture out (it will look quite sticky at this stage) onto a rectangle of cling film (plastic wrap), aiming for a sort of long oblong shape. Place another piece of clingfilm the same size over the top and wrap the sausage completely. Roll it in your hands to smooth out the shape and then twist the ends. Place it in the fridge to chill.

Once solid and nicely firm, unsheath your sausage and dust in icing sugar, and either wrap it in baking parchment if giving it as a gift or, if you want to go the whole hog, tie it up as you would a proper salami. There are some very instructive videos on YouTube about how to tie salami properly, if you are so inclined.

Will keep for up to 1 week, covered, in the fridge.

Note

I use Oro biscuits, which are the Italian equivalent of Rich Teas. If you want to make this fancy, you can use Amaretti. Digestives, Hob Nobs, any kind of basic biscuit will work, really, perhaps just steer clear of pink wafers. Ginger biscuits are also nice.

Marzipan Fruits

It's extraordinary the way culinary traditions travel around the world and end up, who knows how, on our doorsteps and in our kitchens. Every Christmas of my childhood my mum and I made my grandpa a selection of marzipan fruits – little balls of marzipan shaped and painted with food colouring to look like fruit. How these assimilated themselves into our culinary repertoire, I have no idea. It was only when I read about the tradition of *Frutta Martorana* in Sicily that I realised at some point in our family history, someone must have visited the island, seen them *in situ* and stolen the idea.

These miniature marzipan fruits originated at the Monastery of Martorana in Palermo. Legend has it that the Mother Superior ordered her nuns to prepare something special with the almond paste they produced to honour the archbishop during his visit. The nuns created the marzipan fruits and hung them from the trees around the cloisters. Subsequently, they became a traditional gift for children the night before All Saints' Day who would awake to find baskets of marzipan fruits at the foot of their beds, supposedly left for them by their ancestors. Pastry shops all over Sicily now produce the fruits commercially, and one of the most spectacular Sicilian sights is a pastry display case filled with these extraordinarily lifelike fruits, all rendered in such exquisite detail that they seem almost hyper-real.

Once made, if you don't want to eat them these dry and can keep for months, years even. When we made them every year for my marzipan-loving grandpa, he could only bear to eat about half of them, and the rest he kept in a glass cabinet for years and years, to admire and show off to guests.

Makes 12–14 walnut-size fruits of various shapes

150 g (5 oz/1¼ cups) icing (confectioner's) sugar
150 g (5 oz/1½ cups) ground almonds (almond meal)
10 ml (2 tsp) water
10 ml (2 tsp) lemon juice

You will also need

food colouring in different colours (I use concentrated liquid food colouring in a set of 12 colours, widely available online)
a variety of different-size paintbrushes
a few cloves (or plastic/paper leaves and stalks)
12–14 paper cases

Follow the method for making marzipan on p 233 and artfully shape the marzipan into 12–14 fruit shapes of your choice. You can also use ready made marzipan, if you prefer.

Using small paintbrushes, paint the fruits. Brown spots on yellow bananas, the tip of a sharp knife for dimpled orange skin. Scarlet strawberries, purple plums. Place them, once painted and dried, in paper cases. Give away to people you love, or keep them for yourself, if you prefer. They will last for several months in an airtight container, or indefinitely, if you don't want to eat them.

Salted Caramel Truffles

A straightforward process: make a hot caramel sauce, pour onto chopped chocolate, blend, chill, shape and dust in cocoa. As simple and delicious as truffles can ever be. The interior is very luscious, exactly the texture of chocolate Vaseline.

I love to make these as gifts, or for 'after dinner' with coffee. They are always appreciated, especially as I have yet to meet someone who doesn't like salted caramel; whether 'faddy' or not, it is undeniably delicious. Although the salted caramel hurricane has already swept through the UK, it has only just about reached Italy, and you see it as a flavour popping up in *gelaterie*.

Keep in the fridge or a cool place; the texture is at its best when they are cold.

Makes 20

200 g (7 oz) dark chocolate (at least 70 per cent cocoa solids)
100 g (3½ oz/½ cup) sugar
3 tbsp water
pinch of sea salt
15 g (½ oz) butter
100 ml (3½ fl oz/scant ½ cup) double (heavy) cream
cocoa (unsweetened chocolate) powder, for dusting

Blitz the chocolate to small pieces in a food processor (keep it in the processor).

Put the sugar, water and salt in a heavy-based saucepan. Heat over a medium heat, swirling the pan (not stirring the contents), until the sugar has dissolved.

Turn up the heat and allow the syrup to boil away until it begins to change colour. Just as the sugar begins to turn the colour of caramel (a coffee colour is good here – dark, but beware if it starts smoking or smelling of burning), quickly turn down the heat to low and add the butter and cream. Stir well until they are incorporated, then remove from the heat.

Wait for the caramel to stop bubbling (30 seconds or so) then pour it over the chocolate in the processor. Wait a few seconds for the mixture to cool, then blitz the whole lot together until you have a smooth chocolate cream.

Pour into a bowl and chill in the fridge until firm.

Put the cocoa powder on a shallow plate.

Scoop teaspoons of the chilled truffle mixture and roll them between your hands to form 20 balls. Dust the truffles in the cocoa powder and move them around to coat well. Chill until ready to serve.

Panforte

Originally from Siena, the strongest (and least bready) sweet in the sweet Italian canon is the wonderful *Panforte*. Reinforced with a hefty weight of roasted nuts and candied fruit; denser and chewier than a fruitcake, more like nougat's spicier, festive sister, it is one of those things that I never thought of making, as it was so easily bought (even in England) and wrapped in such pretty packaging, too.

The joy of making your own *Panforte* is that you get to control the texture, which should be marvellously giving and chewy, you can choose what you like to put inside it, and you can enjoy its medieval spicy, citrus-scented flavour in all its fresh and festive glory.

This recipe makes one large *Panforte*, but if you make two small ones they are wonderful to give as gifts (as is the big one too, but perhaps for whole families rather than individuals). You can also create your own festive packaging for it.

Serves 8–10

- 30 g (1 oz) butter, plus extra, softened, for greasing
- 200 g (7 oz) almonds (half blanched, half skin-on is nice)
- 40 g (1½ oz) hazelnuts
- 100 g (3½ oz) candied peel (see p 230)
- zest of 1 lemon
- zest of 1 orange
- 100 g (3½ oz/¾ cup, plus 2 tbsp) 00 or plain (all-purpose) flour
- 1 tsp ground cinnamon
- ½ tsp ground nutmeg
- ¼ tsp ground cloves
- ¼ tsp ground pepper (white is traditional, but black is fine)
- 150 g (5 oz) honey
- 150 g (5 oz/⅔ cup) sugar
- pinch of salt
- icing (confectioner's sugar), to dust

Preheat the oven to 170°F (340°F/Gas 3).

Butter a 23 cm (9 in) cake tin with butter and line with baking parchment. Butter the paper too, as this is an exceptionally sticky cake.

Put the almonds and hazelnuts on a baking sheet and toast for 10 minutes until golden. Roughly chop them (very roughly – they can be almost whole, and lots can remain whole) then transfer to a large mixing bowl.

Chop the candied peel into small pieces (no larger than hazelnut size) and add to the bowl. Add the citrus zests, flour and ground spices.

Put the butter, honey, sugar and salt in a saucepan, bring to a simmer and stir until the sugar has melted. Turn up the heat and allow the syrup to just come to a rolling boil.

Pour the syrup into the bowl with the other ingredients and stir well to combine. Pour the batter into the prepared cake tin and transfer to the oven. Cook for 20–25 minutes, or until just golden, then allow to cool completely. When cool, dust with icing sugar. Serve in slices with a strong coffee, or wrap up in lots of greaseproof (waxed) paper and tie with a ribbon to give as a gift.

This keeps well for a week or so in an airtight container.

Panforte possibilities

Add 2 tsp cocoa (unsweetened chocolate) powder to the mix and/or a handful of dried figs for a delicious variation known as *Panforte Scuro* or dark *Panforte*.

Gifts

ESSENTIALS

These are the basics of your *dolci* repertoire, a sort of dessert toolkit if you will. You can use these as the basis for your own creations, adding, adapting and taking away as you see fit.

Candied Peel For Serious People

Real candied peel should be shining, moist and intensely fragrant. It should be decadent and delicious and a little bit magical, to reflect the alchemical process through which it is created. True candying, of both whole fruits and citrus peels, is a process by which the moisture in every cell of the fruit is replaced by sugar, a sweet embalming that guarantees near-infinite preservation. This process happens slowly, by heating the fruit gradually in an ever-more-concentrated sugar syrup. Some candying processes take weeks, some several months. You can tell a true candy because it should glow like a lantern in the light, and be almost totally translucent.

Candying is another gift the Italians inherited from the Arabs, along with sugar itself. The Arabs served candied roses and fruits at the end of lavish meals. I have yet to find a whole candied rose, but if I ever do, I think I will never feel sad again.

This process takes 8–10 days, but you only need to do it once a year (in peak citrus season, in the winter, when you're stuck inside anyway) and each day demands only 20 seconds.

Makes 4 large jars

500 g (1 lb 2 oz) of peel (*cedro* or citron is the best, if you can find it, but I always do orange peel because oranges are so easy to find. Use unwaxed organic fruit if you can.)
1.2 litres (40 fl oz/scant 5 cups) water
1.2 kg (2 lb 11 oz/5½ cups) sugar
100 g (3½ oz) honey

If you want to make this in a natural fashion, eat an orange a day for a few days and you will accumulate enough peel – from around 7–8 large oranges. Keep your peel in a sealed container in the fridge until you have enough.

Peel the oranges using the following method: cut the top and bottom off with a knife, then cut the peel into 4–6 large segments by making incisions down the length of the orange with your knife, and then pulling away the pieces of peel.

Bring a large pan of water to the boil. Add the peel and allow it to boil for a few seconds, then drain it and rinse it under cold water.

Repeat this process twice more (3 boils and rinses in total).

Make a sugar syrup by bringing the water and sugar to the boil in a large pan, stirring once or twice at the beginning to help the sugar dissolve. Once the sugar has dissolved, allow the syrup to boil for 3–4 minutes, then turn off the heat. Drop in your peels and push them down so they are covered with liquid. Cover with a cartouche (see p 255). Set aside overnight.

The following day, bring the whole saucepan just to the boil (complete with cartouche in place). Once just boiling, turn off the heat and set aside.

Repeat this process for at least another 8 days (if using thicker peel – such as *cedro* – you may need 10 days). You can tell they are ready when the peels are completely translucent.

Once they are ready, bring the whole lot just to the boil for a final time and then add the honey (this stops them crystallising). Stir gently to dissolve and then decant the fruit and syrup into sterilised Kilner jars or Tupperware.

The fruit can then be stored in the fridge for a year or more.

Note

There will probably be some extra syrup, which you can keep in a separate jar. I like to use it for brushing buns when they come out of the oven (instead of runny honey) or drizzling on ice creams and things. If you prefer to have the peels without the syrup, you can leave them on a rack over a tray to drain and dry for a day or two until they are tacky but not wet, and then store them this way. At this point they can also be cut into strips and dipped in chocolate.

Cheat's Candied Clementines

A fast, simple way of making quick candied fruit for when you haven't got the time or energy to take the scenic route (see opposite). This method will work for oranges too, though they may take a little longer for their skins to soften, as the rind is tougher and thicker than that of a clementine. You will need a sharp knife to make sure they are sliced nice and thinly.

4 clementines
350 g (12 oz/1⅔ cups) sugar

To candy the clementines, slice them into thin discs (2–3 mm in thickness), put them in a medium saucepan and cover with 570 ml (1 pint) of water. Bring to the boil then drain and discard the water. Pour over the same amount of fresh water and repeat the process.

Add the sugar and another 570 ml (19 fl oz/ scant 2½ cups) of fresh water. Put over a low heat and cook gently for 40–60 minutes, or until the liquid is reduced and the oranges are soft, shiny and candied (keep an eye on them towards the end as they will burn terrifyingly easily).

Pastry Cream
Crema Pasticcera

Pastry cream, or as the French would have it *crème patissiere*, has been in use in Italian dessert tradition since the Renaissance. It is stuffed into croissants and doughnuts, squeezed between layers of sponge to make elaborate, celebratory cakes and sandwiched between biscuits and cookies. It is also used as a filling for tarts, as in the recipe for *Torta della Nonna* (see p 78).

The Italians love this thick, sweet and slightly gloopy cream almost as much as the French do their *crème*, and the English their custard. It is impossible not to love it; the texture is irresistibly thick and wobbly, just asking to be squirted from a doughnut grasped by overly eager fingers, and the flavour is pure, sweet, eggy nostalgia. I love custard in any and all of its manifestations: English, French, Italian – it makes little difference. At cookery school, in true French style (and in accordance with many English recipes too) this pastry cream was always thickened with plain (all-purpose) flour. Here in Italy almost every recipe I have come across uses cornflour (cornstarch). It has the (unintentional) bonus of being gluten free, and the texture is a little more chewy than the plain flour version, but means that the cream holds its own in many cakes and tarts.

The two most common flavourings are lemon and vanilla. I sometimes use both, sometimes only lemon, sometimes only vanilla, depending on what mood I'm in and what the cream is for.

Thick Pastry Cream

This cream is simple, homely and lemon-scented, and thick enough to hold its own in the tart, so that when you cut a slice the custard sandwiched between the two pastry crusts stays firm.

This recipe makes a fairly large quantity, as I like my *Torta* to be amply filled with custard.

Makes enough to fill 1 deep tart such as *Torta della Nonna* (see p 78) (around ¾ litre)

750 ml (25 fl oz/3 cups) milk
4 strips of lemon zest
120 g (4 oz) egg yolk (around 5–6 medium yolks)
120 g (4 oz/½ cup) sugar
65 g (2½ oz/½ cup) cornflour (cornstarch)

Put the milk and strips of lemon zest in a large heavy-based pan over a gentle heat and bring just to a scald. You will see small bubbles appearing at the edge of the pan when it is ready (see p 259). Remove from the heat.

Whisk the yolks with the sugar in a heatproof mixing bowl until pale and mousse-like (you can do this by hand – no need to use a mixer, just a good whisking). Whisk in the cornflour and set aside.

Once the milk is just beginning to simmer, pour it gently in a steady stream over the egg mixture, whisking all the time.

Return the mixture to the pan and cook over a gentle heat, stirring constantly, until you have a thick custard that coats the back of a wooden spoon. You're aiming for the same consistency as thick mayonnaise when it is ready, and it will firm up further once chilled.

Remove the pan from the heat and pour the custard quickly into a container to cool. Remove the lemon zest with tongs (or fingers – but don't burn them). Cover it with clingfilm (plastic wrap) (it should touch the surface of the custard) to prevent it getting a crust and leave it to cool completely.

Lighter Pastry Cream

A slightly looser-set version made with a lower proportion of cornflour (cornstarch). I like to use this one for open fruit tarts or for filling doughnuts. For filling doughnuts I prefer a vanilla version, though you can replace the vanilla pod with some strips of lemon zest if you like.

Makes 500 ml (17 fl oz/2 cups), enough for a fruit tart or 10–12 doughnuts

480 ml (16 fl oz/2 cups) milk
1 vanilla pod (bean), split
4 egg yolks
80 g (3 oz/⅓ cup) sugar
30 g (1 oz/¼ cup) cornflour (cornstarch)
pinch of salt

Follow the method as for Thick Pastry Cream (see opposite), replacing the strips of lemon zest infused in the milk with the split vanilla pod. Once the custard is made, remove the vanilla pod before chilling.

Note

Both of these creams keep well in the fridge for up to 5 days.

Some *crema* possibilities

Add a teaspoon or two of orange blossom water or rose water to your *crema*, or the zest of a Seville orange in the winter, if you're lucky enough to find them. Some strips of orange zest are good too, as is a pinch of powdered saffron for extra yellowness and a whiff of fragrance.

Marzipan

Marzipan, *Pasta Reale*, or *Pasta di Mandorle* as it is also known in Italy, forms the base of some of the most typical and characteristic Italian *dolci*. Its malleability means it is the perfect edible material for expressing culinary creativity, whimsy and artistry, from *Frutta Martorana* (see p 225) to the Sicilian Paschal lamb (an eccentric Easter speciality consisting of marzipan filled with pistachio cream and shaped into a white lamb).

Marzipan is surprisingly easy to make at home. If you do not like the flavour of bitter almonds, using normal almonds mixed only with sugar and liquid will yield a mild, sweet, almondy-tasting result. There are those that argue (like Loredana) that you should always grind the almonds yourself, and preferably peel them too (see p 260). I have used both ready-ground almonds (almond meal) and ground fresh whole ones, and think both have their place.

Makes around 300 g (10½ oz)

150 g (5 oz) blanched almonds, very finely ground in a blender or food processor
150 g (5 oz/1¼ cups) icing (confectioner's) sugar
10 ml (2 tsp) water
10 ml (2 tsp) lemon juice

Mix the finely ground almonds in a bowl with the sugar and most of the water and lemon juice. Knead on a work surface for a few minutes to form a smooth paste. If it looks a touch too dry to knead well, add a drop or two more of water.

Wrap in clingfilm (plastic wrap) and chill or freeze until required.

Nut Brittle

Nut brittle (known as *Gatto/Gateau*) is a popular sweet in Sardinia and in mainland Italy too, where it is usually made with nibbed almonds and served in diamond-shaped pieces with after-dinner coffee, on waxy, perfumed lemon leaves.

Spreading the brittle out with a cut lemon half is a rather romantic (and oddly practical) idea I read about in an old book of *dolci*. The caramel does not stick to the wet surface and the juice in turn adds a lift of lemony freshness to the finished brittle.

I love this brittle made with pine nuts, an inspired idea from one of my favourite English gelato makers, Kitty Travers. You can, however, use any nut you wish.

Serves 6–8

70 g (2½ oz) pine nuts or other nuts of your choice
100 g (3½ oz/½ cup) sugar
1 tsp honey
20 ml (4 tsp) water
15 g (½ oz) butter
pinch of sea salt
½ a lemon

Line a baking sheet with greaseproof paper or a silicone baking mat. Preheat the oven to 170°C (340°F/Gas 3).

Spread the pine nuts (or other nuts) over the base of a baking sheet and toast in the oven for 7 minutes, or until just golden (keep an eye on them – nuts are notoriously awkward and burn fast).

Bring the sugar, honey and water to a boil in a heavy-based saucepan. Keep an eye on it as the liquid starts to bubble and colour. Swirl the pan to help distribute the heat evenly and melt the sugar. After a few minutes of bubbling, the liquid should turn an even caramel colour. Quickly add the butter and continue to boil, swirling the pan every now and then, for 30 seconds to 1 minute, until small bubbles appear and the butter has been homogenised into the mix.

Remove from the heat and stir through the toasted pine nuts and the salt.

Quickly pour the mixture out over the prepared baking sheet or silicone mat and spread flat with the cut half of the lemon.

Allow to cool completely before breaking into shards.

Brittle possibilities

Once made, you can blitz the brittle to a golden dust and sprinkle it on many things. Or simply keep it in shards in an airtight container – it will keep for up to 10 days this way. Serve it with Rosemary *Fior di Latte* (see p 208), or Chocolate Fudge Ice Cream (see p 180).

Sweet Pastry I
Pasta Frolla

This is a rich pastry with a texture and flavour much like a very good buttery biscuit once baked. Because of its high butter content, I use the grating method when lining tart shells with this pastry (see p 236). I find it easier than rolling, and less messy. You can grate the pastry straight from frozen, which means it stays nicely cold. This method also means that when you blind-bake the tart shell you do not have to use ceramic baking beans, or even prick the pastry with a fork to prevent it from puffing up as it bakes. The tart shell bakes 'naked' in the oven, without puffing or shrinkage.

Makes enough for 2 (single-layer) tart shells

350 g (12 oz/2¾ cups) 00 or plain (all-purpose) flour
100 g (3½ oz/¾ cup) icing (confectioner's) sugar
225 g (8 oz) cold butter, roughly diced
good pinch of salt
3 egg yolks

Put the flour, icing sugar, butter and salt in a food processor and pulse to fine breadcrumbs. Add the egg yolks and briefly blend until the mixture comes together as a dough.

Remove from the mixer and shape into two equal rounds. Wrap each round in cling film (plastic wrap) and chill in the fridge or freezer. The dough can be used after 35 minutes of chilling.

Sweet Pastry II

Makes enough for 2 tart bases, or 1 tart base with a lattice top

500 g (1 lb 2 oz/4 cups) 00 or plain (all-purpose) flour
150 g (5 oz/1¼ cups) icing (confectioner's) sugar
300 g (10½ oz) butter
pinch of salt
1 whole egg and 1 egg yolk
zest of 1 lemon

Put the flour, icing sugar, butter and salt in a food processor and pulse until the mixture has the texture of fine breadcrumbs. Add the whole egg, egg yolk and lemon zest and briefly blend until the mixture comes together as a dough.

Remove from the processor and shape into two equal rounds. Wrap each round in cling film (plastic wrap) and chill in the fridge or freezer. The dough can be used after 35 minutes of chilling.

Lining a Tart Shell (grating method)

Take your frozen (or very well chilled) dough and remove it from its wrapping. Grate the pastry into the tart shell, making sure to get a good coverage over the whole base. Using your fingers and the palms of your hand press the pastry into the edges and flatten it over the base, until you have a smooth, even covering. Place in the fridge or freezer to chill for at least 35 minutes.

Blind-baking the tart shell without baking beans

Preheat the oven to 180°C (350°F/Gas 4). Bake the chilled tart shell for around 13 minutes, until golden brown all over. Cool and set aside ready to fill.

Chocolate Pastry

Makes enough for 1 large tart

300 g (10½ oz/2½ cups) 00 or plain (all-purpose) flour
130 g (4 oz/1 cup) icing (confectioner's) sugar
30 g (1 oz/¼ cup) cocoa (unsweetened chocolate) powder
150 g (5 oz) butter
pinch of salt
3 egg yolks

Put the flour, icing sugar, cocoa powder, butter and salt in a food processor then pulse until the mixture has the texture of fine crumbs. Add the egg yolks and pulse the mixture again briefly until it comes together as an even dough. Remove from the mixer and pat it into a rough round, then wrap it in clingfilm (plastic wrap) and chill it in the fridge for at least 30 minutes.

To make the pastry shell, remove the chilled pastry from the fridge and roll it out to a 2 mm thickness, placing it between two sheets of baking parchment if it begins to become too soft and sticky (this will depend on the temperature of your room and hands).

Place the pastry over the tart tin, gently pressing it into the edges and flutes well. Trim the edges to fit the tin.

Put the tart shell in the fridge to rest for 30 minutes.

Preheat the oven to 170°C (340°F/Gas 3). Line the pastry shell with a layer of baking parchment and fill with ceramic baking beans. Blind-bake the shell for 13 minutes, or until crisp and browned at the edges. Remove the baking parchment and baking beans, and return the shell to the oven for another 6 minutes, or until the base is crisp.

Remove from the oven and leave to cool completely before continuing with the recipe.

Mascarpone Cream

Mascarpone is an essential ingredient in many *dolci*. It's easy enough to buy from supermarkets but it's rewarding (and easy) to make your own. (See p 105 for instructions.) This delicious mixture is essentially the same as the filling for *Tiramisù*, but it can also be served as the main event, perhaps with some *Cantucci (see p 27)* for dunking or a biscuit or two. The most indulgent (and possibly the most delicious) way to enjoy it is to serve it at Christmas with slices of *Pandoro* or *Panettone*. It is also good served alongside poached fruit or as a filling for tarts. Like the Ricotta Cream (see p 238) it's hugely versatile. The true joy of it, however, is that it is as good as a thick custard or Pastry Cream (see p 232), if not better, and it doesn't require cooking.

Makes around ½ litre (2 cups)

3 eggs, separated
100 g (3½ oz/½ cup) sugar
500 g (1 lb 2 oz) mascarpone

Whisk the egg yolks and sugar in the bowl of a stand mixer (or in a mixing bowl using an electric beater) until pale, thick and mousse-like. Fold in the mascarpone gently.

In a clean bowl and with clean beaters, whisk the egg whites until they form smooth peaks, then gently fold them into the yolk and mascarpone mixture. Cover and refrigerate until ready to use.

Serve in little glasses or bowls, alongside slices of *Panettone* or biscuits.

Some nice additions

Fold through a tablespoon of rum or the zest of an orange at the end, or add the scraped seeds from a vanilla pod (bean).

Mascarpone Icing

This is the topping for the Spiced Pumpkin Cake (see p 102), and is a great icing to have up your sleeve for all sorts of other desserts.

Makes enough for 1 sandwich-style cake (to ice top and middle)

100 g (3½ oz/¾ cup) icing (confectioner's) sugar
180 g (6½ oz) full-fat Philadelphia cream cheese
250 g (9 oz) mascarpone
zest of 1 orange or 1 lemon plus 1 tbsp juice

Sieve the icing sugar into a mixing bowl to remove lumps, add the other cream cheese, mascarpone and lemon/orange zest and juice, and stir well to make a smooth icing. Cover and refrigerate until ready to use.

Ricotta Cream (made with cream)

This is a useful thing for filling pastries, doughnuts and large tarts. Use it to fill a prepared sweet pastry case, then top with fresh fruit or berries. Adding the cream lightens the flavour and the texture.

Makes enough to fill one large tart

500 g (1 lb 2oz) ricotta
150 g (5 oz/1¼ cups) icing (confectioner's) sugar
250 ml (8½ fl oz/1 cup) double (heavy) cream
vanilla or zest of 1 lemon (optional)

Beat the ricotta and the icing sugar together in a mixing bowl until smooth and creamy. In a separate mixing bowl, whip the cream to form stiff peaks. Fold the cream through the ricotta, cover and chill until ready to use.

Ricotta Cream (made without cream)

A pure, sweetened ricotta cream is the base of so many Italian *dolci*, and the filling for *Cannoli* (see p 160). This is such a simple combination and is a substantial element in the finished sweet, so it is important that the ricotta is of good quality, preferably sheep's milk. To this you can add any other flavourings you wish, such as vanilla, lemon zest, orange zest or Amaretto.

Makes around 500g (1 lb 2oz)

500 g (1 lb 2oz) ricotta
130 g (4 oz/⅔ cup) caster (superfine) sugar
pinch of salt

Beat all the ingredients together in a mixing bowl until smooth. Chill until ready to use.

Lemon Glaze Icing

It's hard to give a precise recipe for lemon glaze icing, the kind of simple, tangy white one that (just) dribbles down the side of so many wonderful cakes. This quantity makes a relatively stiff one, which will dribble only *very* slightly, and remain thick and white and opaque, and form the defined crest of your cake rather than a sheen.

Makes enough to ice 1 large cake

250 g (9 oz/2 cups) icing (confectioner's) sugar
30–40 ml (2–3 tbsp) lemon juice

Put the icing sugar in a bowl. Add 30 ml (2 tbsp) of the lemon juice and mix thoroughly, adding more juice depending on your desired texture.

If you want a thinner, translucent glaze that soaks into the cake more, add another teaspoon of lemon juice, and continue to add juice to make it as runny as you wish. This will provide more of a general shine rather than a defined icing. You can tinker with it as you see fit – there are truly 50 shades of glaze.

Fatless Sponge *Pan di Spagna*

Pan di Spagna – literally translated as 'Spanish bread' – is a basic form of sponge cake made without fat. An inheritance from the Spanish rule of Sicily, it forms the base of many sweet cakes and desserts all over Italy. It is a simple, light, buttercup-yellow and fluffy sponge cake, very delicately flavoured and textured, and made without any additional raising agent – its height derives entirely from the air incorporated into the eggs by whisking. It is an extremely useful recipe to have up your sleeve, and freezes well, so you can defrost it any time you want to make *cassata*, trifle, or even just to serve as a simple sponge square alongside some poached fruit and cream.

The method is unbelievably easy – you simply let the mixer do all the work for you. The whole assembly takes about 10 minutes.

Serves 8–10

melted butter, for greasing
5 eggs
150 g (5 oz/⅔ cup) sugar
75 g (2½ oz/½ cup plus 2 tbsp) potato flour
75 g (2½ oz/½ cup plus 2 tbsp) 00 or plain (all-purpose) flour, plus extra to dust
pinch of salt

Using a pastry brush, grease a 24 cm (9½ in) spring-form cake tin with melted butter and lightly dust with flour.

Preheat the oven to 170°C (340°F/Gas 3). Beat the eggs with the sugar (either in a stand mixer or in a mixing bowl using a handheld electric whisk) for 3–5 minutes, until pale, very fluffy and almost mousse-like. When you lift the whisk there should be obvious ribbons of the mixture that keep their shape for a few seconds.

Add the flours and the salt, and fold gently to incorporate, being careful not to knock out too much air from the mixture but simultaneously being careful to stir through the flours evenly.

Pour the mixture gently into the prepared tin, smoothing the top.

Bake for 40–45 minutes until golden.

Remove and allow to cool in the tin for at least 10 minutes before turning out to cool on a wire rack and using as required.

PRESERVES

Preserves are potted memories, the clue to their true purpose exemplified in their name. There is no other food that encapsulates a season, or the distinct flavour and sensuality of a season, in quite the same way. This is partly why making preserves appeals to me so much: locking in the sun, the ripe flavour of fruit at its best to enjoy throughout the year. Jars of potted summer sweetness can then sit patiently, waiting for the next time you break open a warm scone, or slice the crust from a fresh loaf.

Known as *marmellata* in Italy, a term which describes both citrus preserves (which we in England would call marmalade) and stone fruit/berry conserves, jam is popular in Italy as a filling for the ubiquitous *Crostata* or to spread on toast at breakfast. As fruit here is so abundant and of such high quality, it is hard not to make delicious jam.

Good jam is not difficult or complicated to make, but there are a few things to consider if you want to make sure your jam is truly exceptional. Here are my essentials for good jam making.

Lemon

I add a good amount of lemon to almost every jam I make. Lemon helps bring out the best in the fruit and also contributes pectin, which helps the jam set. This is especially important in fruit that is low in pectin, such as strawberries.

Less sugar

Though traditional jam recipes call for equal quantities of fruit and sugar, this was to ensure the keeping properties of the jam, as sugar is a preservative. A jam made with this quantity of sugar will no doubt keep longer, but will taste much less of the fruit. Preserves traditionally contain less sugar and more fruit, so it is perhaps more technically correct to call my jam recipes 'preserves' rather than 'jams', as I tend to aim for half sugar to fruit (or just over half if I am using tart fruit and adding lemon).

Storage

Adding less sugar to jams (as I do) means they are less likely keep for long periods of time. A high-sugar jam can be kept for up to a year. I prefer to make the compromise in order to have fresh, bright-tasting jams and to eat them faster (which is no great hardship). For this reason, I keep all my jams in the fridge or in a cold place. Even with these low quantities of sugar, these jams will keep for a good 6 months.

Macerating

I tend to make all my jams using the following method: the fruit is macerated with sugar and lemon juice, then brought to a simmer. This initial maceration coaxes out the very best in the fruit, and dissolves the sugar too, so that by the time you come to cooking it the fruit has already collapsed and is suspended in a clear syrup. The remaining cooking time is just to evaporate water and reduce that syrup to a setting point, without losing the intense, fresh flavour of the fruit.

Sterilisation

To sterilise your jars: wash them well in hot soapy water, rinse, then put them in a baking tray (pan) in a low oven for 20 minutes. Remove and allow to cool.

Setting point

I use the saucer method to check for setting point. Place a saucer in the fridge. Dribble a little of the jam you are making onto the cold saucer. Wait 10–20 seconds and then push the blob of jam with your finger. If wrinkles appear on the surface of the jam, then your jam is ready to pot. If not, return it to the heat and cook for a few minutes longer. I prefer a softer set and this method ensures that my jams still dribble rather than sit in a solid lump.

Jam & Ricotta

As hot toast with butter and jam is one of my favourite things in the world it has been a blow to discover that this phenomenon does not exist in Italian culture. The culture of toast is a very different one; while some people toast fresh bread, many Italian 'toast' breakfasts are instead composed of *fette biscotatte*, a sort of rusk, or twice-baked bread which is bought ready-made in packets. This is dry and crisp, without the soft interior give of chewy dough so central to the concept of fresh toast, and rarely spread with butter, though sometimes with jam, honey or marmalade. The culture of adding both butter and jam does not seem to exist at all, and when I talk fondly of such things my rhapsodies are often met with scowls of disapproval.

Rather than try to implement this combination, which has been lost in translation, I have instead become a habitual eater of toast with jam and ricotta. Ricotta and jam make a very happy pairing, the creamy, only slightly cheesy richness of the ricotta cut through with the fresh, tart, fruity hit of the jam. It's a truly excellent breakfast, one I recommend trying.

Apricot & Lavender Jam

I love this pairing, which I discovered in Caroline Rimbert Craig's *Provence: The Cookbook.* It is a combination that conjures up the heady days at the start of summer, and it felt especially fitting to make here in Sardinia, as my lavender plant is one of the few things to survive my devastating ability to destroy every plant I purchase, and as the local apricots are of such extraordinary quality and profligacy. The lavender adds a fragrant and almost savoury musk, which highlights the tart, floral nature of the fruit.

Makes 2 jars

500 g (1 lb 2oz) apricots
juice of 1 lemon
370 g (13 oz/1⅔ cups) sugar
sprig of lavender

Cut the apricots in half and remove the stones. (Dry these, then crack them open; inside are the bitter almonds you can use to make *Amaretti*, p 34). Put the apricot halves in a bowl.

Place two small saucers in the fridge (to test for setting point).

Squeeze the lemon juice over the apricots. then pour over the sugar. Transfer to a jam pan or deep, heavy-based saucepan, add the lavender sprig and bring to the boil.

Simmer gently for around 20 minutes. Spoon a little of the jam onto one of the cold saucers. Wait a few seconds and then push it with your finger. If wrinkles appear on the surface of the jam, then your jam is ready to pot. If not, cook for a few minutes longer and check again. Remove from the heat when setting point has been reached.

Pick out and discard the lavender sprig. Pot the hot jam in sterilised jars (see opposite) and seal well. Allow to cool, then keep in the fridge. Eat with toast and butter, with toast and ricotta, with yoghurt or with pancakes.

Apricot Jam

I love all jam but this jam is special. It's not fancy or fiddly or innovative. There are no special tricks or funky ingredients. I don't even add lemon to this one. The secret, and perhaps you will hate me for this, is simply to use really good fruit.

You cannot make really good jam with poor fruit. This jam, which uses nothing other than good fruit and sugar, is testament to that fact. Pellegrino Artusi – an Italian businessman with excellent moustaches and the author of a seminal work on Italian cooking, *La Scienza in Cucina e L'arte di Mangiar Bene* – whose recipe this is based on, states in his introduction that the belief that sub-par fruit will cook into good jam is an error, and he is right (about almost everything, as it turns out).

Apricots in England are often sad things: mushy, uniformly orange and lacking in flavour. Try to find some that have been grown somewhere warm, and are blushed and freckled by the sun, and heady with fragrance. Here in Sardinia, I feel very lucky to be able to get hold of good, local, fresh apricots, laden with scent, blushing pink and speckled with russet freckles. Smaller and with furrier coats than their imported relatives, they have a wonderfully intense flavour perfect for this jam.

Makes 3–4 large jars

1.2 kg (2½ lb) ripe apricots
600 g (1lb 5 oz/2¾ cups) sugar

Wash and halve the apricots and reserve their stones. Place two small saucers in the fridge (to test for setting point; see p 240).

Put the fruit and their stones in a deep, heavy-based saucepan or jam pan and bring to a simmer over a low heat. You don't need to add water, just stir them occasionally and keep an eye on them to make sure the fruit doesn't stick to the bottom of the pan. Cook gently for 20–30 minutes, until the fruit is soft and collapsing.

Pass the fruit through a sieve or *mouli,* and return the pureé to the pan (no need to wash the pan). Add the sugar and cook for 20 minutes, stirring constantly. Spoon a little of the jam onto one of the cold saucers. Wait a few seconds and then push it with your finger. If wrinkles appear on the surface of the jam, then it is ready to pot. If not, cook for a few minutes longer and check again. Remove from the heat when setting point has been reached.

Pot the hot jam in sterilised jars (see p 240) and seal well. Allow to cool, then keep in the fridge for up to 6 months.

Citrus Curd

This is a lovely thing to make on a wet winter afternoon to steam up your windows and make the whole house smell tantalisingly of citrus and butter.

It is much less effort than it seems, and requires only 20 minutes or so of attention. I like to make jars in time to give as gifts for Christmas; the citrus season coincides with Christmas preparations, and it seems a wonderful way of capturing Italy's signature citrus in jars and sending (or taking) it home to my English family.

You can use other combinations of citrus as you please.

Makes 4 jars

4 lemons
3 clementines
1 small orange
3 whole eggs
5 egg yolks
250 g (9 oz/1 cup plus 2 tbsp) sugar
200 g (7 oz) unsalted butter, cut into pieces

Zest and juice the fruit (you should have 300 ml/10 fl oz/1¼ cups of juice in total).

Combine the juice, zest, eggs, egg yolks and sugar in a bowl, then transfer to a medium saucepan set over a low heat.

Cook, whisking, until the sugar has melted (about 4 minutes), then add half the butter. Turn up the heat to medium and continue cooking and whisking until the butter has been incorporated. Add the rest of the butter and continue cooking and whisking for a further 8–10 minutes, until the mixture starts to bubble then remove from the heat.

Strain through a fine sieve and decant into sterilised jars (see p 240) and seal well. Allow to cool, then store in the fridge for up to two weeks.

Fig Jam

The flavour of a fig is hard to define, somewhere between freshly cut grass, rain, sap and sugar, and when eaten from the tree, their sun-warmed flesh collapsing in the mouth into seeds and syrup, they are truly ambrosial. Their flavour, captured in a jar of jam, is more musky and dark, more fig-roll, wet earth and store-cupboards, a flavour that's as content on buttered toast as it is spooned alongside a slab of fresh ricotta. The colour is a deep, rich berry-wine, with flurries of seeds speckled throughout like stars in a clear night sky.

Makes 4 jars

1 kg (2 lb 4 oz) fresh, ripe figs
600 g (1 lb 5 oz/2¾ cups) granulated sugar
1 large lemon

Wash the figs and remove the stalks. Cut them into quarters.

Place the figs, along with the sugar, in a deep, heavy-based saucepan or jam pan. Cut the lemon into quarters, remove any pips with a knife and discard. Squeeze the lemon wedges over the figs and sugar, then drop in the squeezed pieces too.

Stir the whole lot, cover, and leave in a cool place to macerate, preferably overnight, or for at least a few hours.

Remove the lemon pieces from the pan and discard.

Place two saucers in the fridge (to test for setting point).

Cook the jam at a low simmer for around 40 minutes, stirring occasionally. Check the set by spooning a little jam onto a cold saucer, waiting 10–20 seconds, and then pushing the jam with your finger. If you see wrinkles form, then the jam will set.

If the jam has not reached setting point, continue to cook for another 10–20 minutes, then check again. Remove from the heat when setting point has been reached.

Pot the jam while still hot in sterilised jars (see p 240) and seal well. Allow to cool, then store in the fridge for up to six months.

Strawberry Jam

Strawberry jam is indisputably the most precious of all the jams. It has a floral delicacy and sweet intensity that is incomparable. This is the best strawberry jam recipe I have ever made. It allows the berries to maintain their integrity, not cooked so much so that they disintegrate or are muffled by the solid shout of sugar; instead entire and flavourful and suspended in a shining fragrant syrup, almost like candied strawberries.

To counterbalance the sweetness of the strawberries, a lot of lemon is added and the tiniest pinch of salt too. The butter is a trick from my cooking school days, which helps to dissolve the scum on the top of the jam, and (I think) adds a subtle edge to the flavour.

Makes 6 jars

1.2 kg (2½ lb) best strawberries
800 g (1 lb 12 oz/3⅔ cups) sugar
2 lemons
small pinch of salt
hazelnut-size piece of butter

The night before you want to make your jam, wash, hull and halve the strawberries and put them in a large bowl. Pour over the sugar, cut the lemons into quarters (discarding any pips), squeeze the juice over the fruit then drop the lemon shells into the bowl too. Stir the whole lot a few times, then cover and leave overnight to macerate.

The next day, sterilise your jars (see p 240) Place two small saucers in the fridge (to test for setting point).

Remove and discard the lemons from the bowl of strawberries. Transfer the fruit and the juice from the bowl into a deep, heavy-based saucepan or jam pan and bring to the boil. Simmer for 10 minutes.

Spoon a little of the jam onto one of the cold saucers. Wait a few seconds, then push it with your finger. If wrinkles appear on the surface of the jam then your jam is ready to pot. If not, cook for a few minutes longer. Remove from the heat when setting point has been reached. Add the butter and the pinch of salt and stir gently to dissolve the scum that forms on top. Ladle into your prepared jars and seal well. Allow to cool, then keep in the fridge for up to 6 months.

NOTES ON INGREDIENTS

Abbamele

A traditional Sardinian product also known as *sapa di miele.* After the honeycomb is drained of honey it is broken up and boiled in water, then strained and the resulting liquid (a mixture of pollen and remaining honey) is cooked gently and reduced to a dark syrup. The flavour is deliciously complex, with a very slight bitterness, reminiscent of coffee, caramel, pollen and beeswax. If you can find it, I recommend trying it drizzled on ricotta, with a slab of good pecorino or on thick yoghurt. It is also very good drizzled over the Rosemary *Fior di Latte* (see p 208).

Almonds

Almonds grow all over Italy, and have been cultivated and exported from Sicily for centuries. In Sicily they are celebrated in the infamous almond granita, which is a traditional breakfast. Here in Sardinia good local almonds are easy to find and inexpensive to buy. They usually have to be peeled but the flavour is extraordinary.

Bitter almonds

These are covered in detail on page 34. They are fairly difficult to get hold of depending on where you are, but can sometimes be bought from health food shops or online, occasionally sold as 'apricot kernels'. If you cannot find them, you can use normal almonds and add a drop or two of almond essence.

Butter

All butter in Italy is unsalted, so by default I use only unsalted. If you wish to use salted butter, then omit the salt from the recipes. See also *Lard and Butter.*

Candied fruit

While I have included recipes for candying oranges (see p 230–231), there are many other types of candied fruit (and candied pumpkin) available, which are worth seeking out if you are a *canditi* enthusiast. Their stained glass beauty is a joy to look at even if you never use them in your cooking. A mixture of candied fruit is ideal for many sweet Italian recipes, and essential to decorate *Cassata* (see p 88). They are widely available online, though for the real thing it is worth taking a trip (even if only virtual) to Pietro Romanengo, Italy's oldest artisanal confectioners, just outside Genoa. I have wasted many hours browsing their online shop, but have yet to get there in person.

Chocolate

All the chocolate I use is dark chocolate, known as *fondente* in Italy. If you can find it, aim for 70 per cent cocoa solids or above. As is also true with cooking and drinking wine, don't use chocolate in cooking you wouldn't be happy eating.

Chocolate chips

Lots of pastries in Italy contain chocolate chips, but I find them difficult to come by when making my own recipes. I also find them often a bit stale-tasting, so I prefer to chop up bars of chocolate into small pieces for recipes that call for chips. If you have a brand of chips you like, by all means use them.

Citrus fruit

It will come as little surprise to anyone who has visited Italy that the citrus fruit is some of the best in the world. However, I hadn't really taken into account how serious the difference was between the citrus fruit we get in most shops in England and the stuff that is widely available here. The size varies wildly – exported lemons are often tiny, which will affect your finished recipes. Try to buy large, unwaxed organic lemons and oranges, if you can.

Cocoa powder

Cocoa powder (unsweetened chocolate powder) should always be unsweetened, occasionally labelled in Italy as *amaro*.

Coffee

I buy and use standard Lavazza espresso coffee, in all my cooking and coffee-drinking life. I'm sure plenty of coffee fanatics will frown upon this, but I like the happy red packets, and it's cheap.

Cornflour (Cornstarch)

*A*n essential ingredient in *crema rinforzata* and many other Italian *dolci*.

Cream

All the recipes included here are made with simple, straightforward Italian cream, which will translate to a single (half and half) cream. You can use double (cream) or whipping cream.

Cream cheese

Good old Philadelphia cream cheese is easily found here in Italy, perhaps thanks to the national love of cheesecake. Use the full-fat variety, rather than the lower-fat one, as it behaves differently and has a much thinner consistency when whipped. Always pour off and discard the liquid that sits at the top of the pack.

Eggs

Eggs are always medium and free-range, unless specified otherwise. Try to find eggs with a nice, deep-orange yolk, which in Italy is known fittingly as the *rosso*, or the 'red' of the egg. These will ensure your cakes, custards and tarts have a beautiful saffron-yellow hue.

Fabbri amarena cherries

Amarena cherries are small sour cherries that grow mostly in Bologna and Modena. Gennaro Fabbri and his wife Rachele began producing these cherries cooked in syrup commercially at the beginning of the 20th century. The couple took over the general store in Portomaggiore behind which was an orchard of wild cherries. Rachele began cooking the cherries in syrup, bottling and selling them, and thus the Fabbri company was born. The company is still family-run, and the white and blue ceramic jar decorated in Art-Nouveau style has become an icon of Italian food culture, and something I collect for myself too, to keep paintbrushes and pens in. The cherries are used in many gelatos and pastries, and have a flavour, scent and appearance that is utterly irresistible. For any sweet enthusiast, they are well worth seeking out.

Farro

Raw emmer wheat grains which are used in savoury and sweet recipes in Italy. This is the grain to use for the filling for the *Pastiera Napoletana* on page 50 if you are starting from scratch rather than using *grano cotto*.

Fennel seeds

Fennel seeds are one of the few spices used frequently in Italian cookery. I love the grassy, aniseed back-note they provide, and the clean, almost medicinal fragrance, which works so well after rich, savoury food. When buying them, the greener the colour the fresher they tend to be. You should be able to smell the difference too. Fresh ones have a much more citrus-sharp note, whereas the brown, faded ones smell more like old cumin.

Flour

00 Flour

The softest, most refined white flour, used in cakes and as an Italian equivalent of plain (all-purpose) flour. You can substitute all the 00 flour in every recipe with plain/all-purpose white flour.

0 Flour (Manitoba)

The Italian equivalent of strong white bread flour, with a higher gluten content, used for making bread. Named after the region in Canada where most of the wheat is grown.

Chestnut flour

A wonderful, toasty, smoky, pale-brown flour that is widely available in Italy and should be in England too. It has the most amazing autumnal forest flavour, and is worth seeking out to make the Dark Chocolate, Chestnut and Hazelnut Cantucci (see p 28).

Semola

Finely ground durum wheat flour, pale golden and slightly sandy in texture, this is used to make pasta and also in some of my baking recipes. It is sometimes labelled as 'semolina flour' or 'semolata'.

Gelatine

I use leaf gelatine rather than powder. The leaves are now widely available, and are much easier to work with than any other form. The leaves vary slightly in size so I have specified weight in grams also.

Grano Cotto

Cooked wheat grains, which are found in shops in Italy (and sometimes in the UK too) and sold almost exclusively for use in *pastiera*. The cooked grain generally comes in a jar, and is often quite salty so may need a quick rinse and drain before use.

Herbs

All herbs should be fresh. The only herb I use dried is bay. Herbs make wonderful additions to sweet things, and it is well worth cultivating a few on a window ledge if you can.

Lard (*strutto*) and butter

Lard is still used in many traditional Italian baked goods. In Sardinia particularly almost all traditional biscuits, breads, tarts and pastries are made with lard. This is because of the tradition of pig-rearing which meant that lard (probably homemade) was more widely available and cheaper than butter. In the north of Italy, where cattle are reared on a larger scale, butter production is a large industry, but in Sardinia the landscape is generally unsuited to dairy farming, so butter is not a major part of the diet. Having said that, near me in Oristano there is an area called Arborea, which was previously marshland, and was drained by the Fascist government in the 1920s. A commune then sprang up mostly populated by farming families from the Veneto, who brought with them their agricultural practices and their dishes, too (there is a yearly polenta festival). Here, lush green grass grows and dairy farming is a major industry. The brand Arborea, which makes milk, butter, yoghurt and cheese, now exports all over Italy. I have visited one of the farms and the animal welfare is extraordinary; when not grazing open pasture the cows are kept in spacious pens where they are cooled by giant fans and entertained by rotating scratching posts and large speakers that play classical music.

Lard in the kitchen

Butter is a wonderful ingredient that imparts cakes, biscuits, tarts and pastries with an undeniably delicious flavour, but there is a friable quality that lard gives that is even more pronounced than when using butter (only just, but still). There are purists that will only use lard in many traditional recipes, and I can see their point, as it does seem to make things more crisp. However, if you are a vegetarian or dislike using lard you can easily replace it with butter.

Lievito

Italian baking powder, *lievito*, is a magical thing that comes in sachets ready to go. The sachets are for some reason always daintily decorated in truly kitsch style depicting cherubs, angels or little girls with pigtails. Each sachet contains 16 g (½ oz) of *lievito*, which seems to work just right for one cake. I have substituted it with 1 tablespoon of equivalent baking powder.

Mascarpone

A thick, smooth, luscious cream cheese, mascarpone originates from the northern Italian region of Lombardia, and is the traditional dairy element in the ubiquitous Italian dessert, *Tiramisù*. The real thing, made by hand, is something I have never been lucky enough to encounter, but the supermarket pasteurised stuff is a safe and sound fall-back. Made by coagulating cream with an acidic element such as lemon juice, mascarpone imparts a rich, smooth creaminess to anything it is added to. The delicate dairy element of cheesiness is slightly more pronounced than in a standard cream, which is why mascarpone does battle so well with strong flavours such as coffee, or very floral flavours such as strawberry. It's a little feistier, and has a bit more to say for itself than standard, fluffy-light whipped cream, and for that reason deserves a place in every sweet-lover's fridge.

Mascarpone should be easy to find in most major supermarkets, or you can very easily make mascarpone at home (see p 105).

Milk

I use full-fat milk in all of the recipes.

Nuts

When buying nuts for use in baking, it is important that they are fresh. Check for sealed foil packaging, which generally keeps them better. If buying blanched nuts this is particularly important, as they lose their flavour and become stale faster.

Orange blossom water

A good orange blossom water is not always easy to find. It needs to have a strong scent, and preferably to be kept in the fridge to retain its potency.

Pandoro

This traditional Italian sweet brioche can be found in many Italian delis and in some supermarkets. It makes a decadent alternative to trifle sponges in the Quince, Bay, Marsala & Hazelnut Trifle recipe on page 132.

Ricotta

I have written extensively about ricotta, which type to use and when on pages 76–77.

Salt

I add salt to almost every sweet thing I make, excluding fruit sorbets, creams and custards. It balances the sweetness and provides a more rounded flavour. Salt is an especially important ingredient in all desserts and cakes containing nuts or chocolate, as it helps to cut through the richness and fat. It is also essential in gelato.

Almost all gelato in Italy contains salt, which is one of the reasons it is so delicious and why it makes you so thirsty (I always need to drink lots of water after gelato). It's essential to round off the sweetness and cut through the cream. I use a simple fine sea salt in all my cooking.

Sprinkles

A sad life it would be without sprinkles. I have to admit I'd completely forgotten about them until I saw them on so many *dolci* here in Sardinia – even on the most traditional ones. Find the most colourful ones you can and add them to anything you feel like.

Sugar

Brown sugars rarely feature in Italian baking, and by default almost all the recipes in this book feature simple, white granulated sugar. I don't even buy caster (superfine) sugar – I've never seen it for sale here – but either caster or granulated is fine. There are only one or two recipes in the book that call for brown sugar, and in these the toffee flavour is essential. All sugar is thus white granulated unless specified otherwise.

Vanilla

Real vanilla seeds from a real vanilla pod are very, very precious things. Vanilla pods are formidably expensive here in Sardinia, so I tend to save them for something really special, and I use a good extract for everything else. Many Italian pastries contain vanillin, a sort of fake vanilla which smells very strongly and sweetly, and which you will no doubt have caught a whiff of frequently as you walk past bars in Italy. Equally, a lot of the commercially available baking powder is pre-flavoured with this synthetic vanillin. There's no denying real vanilla is incomparable. Its musky sweetness is a Madagascan rainforest away from the stuff injected into this baking powder, but to my sentimental heart, both have their charms and their place.

Yeast

I always use fresh yeast, as I much prefer it and find it easier and more efficient to work with. Luckily it is readily available here in Italy, but should now be pretty easy to find (try in health food shops). If you can't find it, dried yeast is fine. Just beware that the quantities of dried yeast versus fresh are exactly half: so for 10 g fresh yeast use 5 g dried.

Yoghurt

Always use full-fat natural yoghurt, the texture and flavour of which is best for baking and eating. In baking, yoghurt adds moistness to cakes, contributing to a tender crumb and a sharp, tart flavour.

The drinks cupboard

In my imagination I have a drinks cupboard, as my dad did when I was growing up. It's stuffed full of ancient bitters and liqueurs with faded labels and the unmistakable smell of damp wood and alcohol, like a pub basement. In reality I have half of a kitchen cupboard devoted to a few bottles that I use regularly. The drinks cupboard should ideally contain:

Marsala: I use dry

Campari: indisputable

Brandy: occasional and for Christmas

Red & white wine: for everything

Amaretto: Disaronno – I love the bottle too

Prosecco: you never know… and also for jelly

Alchermes: a spiced liqueur, useful if you love to make traditional Italian *dolci*, and also worth having just for the bottle.

EQUIPMENT LIST

I have split this list into what I think is essential and what is optional. However, the 'essential' list should be taken with a pinch of salt, as even I could never claim that a bundt tin was essential to anyone. But if you like baking and making sweet things, and you are an enthusiast rather than a professional, I would say these are items you may well like to have in your kitchen.

The optional list details things you might like to have if you want to attempt the more detailed recipes in this book, which I urge you to do. Perhaps you will only make *Cannoli* at home once a year or so, but it will be a joyous day when you do, and a *Cannoli* tube or two is not a great expenditure, and they don't take up much space. You can also lend them to friends who might like to have a go.

Essential

Cake tins

I use the following cake tins: 2 × shallow Victoria sandwich tins measuring 22 cm (8½ in) width; a deep spring-form cake tin measuring 23 cm (9 in).

Bundt tin(s)

For some reason, almost every basic homeware shop, DIY or hardware shop I have been into in Sardinia has a wide range of reasonably priced bundt tins. A handful of classic Italian cakes are traditionally made in these. You can find the simple, smooth, wide doughnut-shaped ones, or more intricate fluted variations. I own a selection of both. They are also very good for making jellies, and for giant *Panna Cottas* should you wish to. My bundt tins are all 23 cm (9 in) width.

Fancy cake tin

I was lucky enough to be gifted a fancy Charlotte tin from Nordicware, which is one of my most prized possessions. It is extremely useful for making plain cakes look fancy, and everyone should own at least one.

Fluted tart shell with removable base

I use this for almost every tart I make, particularly for the Chocolate and Mascarpone Tart with Blackberries and Sage (see p 54).

Tart tin with straight sizes

These are more easily found in Italy than in England, but if you can't find one you can use a spring-form cake tin. When making a *crostata* I often use this, as it gives a more rustic, straight-sided crust. You can make any of the tart recipes in this tin, but I prefer the fluted edges for the more fancy tarts.

Flat baking sheet

For baking scones, buns and biscuits I prefer a simple flat sheet without sides.

Rectangular baking tray (pan)

With a slightly raised edge for recipes such as *Schiacciata* (see p 170).

Small serrated knives

These are underrated and to me, invaluable. They are also cheap and incredibly versatile. I like those made by Victorinox, but I also have a few I have picked up in the weekly market in Oristano. Useful for slicing anything small, awkwardly shaped or slippery – which is many things.

At least one very sharp knife

In contrast to the above, this is what you will need when slicing/dicing/cutting anything large and cumbersome, like a quince or an apple. It does not have to be fancy or expensive, as long as it is kept sharp.

Swivel peeler

Also known as a Y-shaped peeler this is the only kind of peeler I use or trust. It is much more effective and easy to use than any other shape or size. A simple, utilitarian stainless steel one is always best.

Metal and glass mixing bowls

For melting chocolate or anything that requires a *bain-marie* (see p 255).

Microplane graters

These are really worth buying, especially as so many recipes in this book call for citrus zest.

Bread scraper/dough scraper

Metal or plastic, these are invaluable tools in the kitchen. I like the plastic ones for baking, as they are flexible and can be used as a spatula, too, for scraping out bowls. The rigid metal ones are better for cutting dough. One of each is ideal.

Small sieve

For icing (confectioner's) sugar dusting, something which is required for a surprising number of Italian *dolci*.

Large sieve

For straining custards. I almost never sieve flour these days. Flour is now so refined (and weevil-free) that it almost never needs sifting. Occasionally icing (confectioner's) sugar or cocoa (unsweetened chocolate) powder might need sifting if they have become lumpy.

Digital scale

I can no longer live or cook without a digital scale. I highly recommend investing in one. They are not expensive and make measuring much easier.

Rolling pin

A good long one, for rolling things.

Pastry brushes

The silicone ones don't work well, even if they are more hygienic and easier to wash up. A good old-fashioned wooden one with bristles is best.

Strand of spaghetti

Without doubt one of the greatest and most pleasurable discoveries I have ever made is that instead of ruining cakes by plunging a knife into the centre to see if they're done, or searching for hours in vain for that metal skewer you bought specially and can never locate, you can use a strand of spaghetti from your spaghetti jar (or just from a packet). Plunge the strand of spaghetti into the centre of the cake and if it comes out clean, the cake is cooked through. Genius of the most satisfactory kind.

Optional

Silicone baking mats

I own one of these from my days of serious baking, and they are very useful. Things stick less to them than to baking parchment, and they prevent you constantly using and discarding the parchment too. They are very easy to wash, essentially wipe-clean.

Tiny spatula

The tiny spatula is a great thing. Useful for applying and smoothing icing, for lifting and scraping, it is the unsung hero of the pastry kitchen. It is also undeniably cute and fits snugly in an apron pocket.

Tiny whisk

The tiny whisk is a great feat of design, and something I have used since my cookery school days, where it was known as a 'sauce whisk'. For whisking small quantities (such as an egg wash for buns) it is extremely useful. You can, of course, use a fork, but it is less ergonomic and considerably less aesthetically interesting.

The KitchenAid: a digression

Life with a KitchenAid or other type of stand mixer is better. It is the original hands-free device. It will save you time, effort and most essentially, it will give you back your hands. Just think of all those things your hands can be doing while the KitchenAid works away: playing with your phone, stroking the cat, wiping surfaces!

Some pieces of equipment can truly make the difference between dread and enjoyment in the kitchen. Prior to the KitchenAid, I dreaded making cakes.

I'm not saying you need a KitchenAid. They take up a fair amount of space and are inescapably expensive. Equally, I'm not saying that you can't be an amazing baker without one, or make delicious and wonderful things without it, because you can. But, if you are serious about baking, but also serious about timesaving, as I am, then I would say you need this machine in your kitchen.

Blender

I own and use regularly both a jug blender and a handheld stick blender. Though the stick blender is invaluable and enormously versatile, for certain tasks, such as grinding nuts, it simply can't cope. Thankfully, in most scenarios you can either chop the nuts by hand, or buy ready-ground almonds (almond meal).

Pestle and mortar

This is an invaluable tool in the kitchen, and for grinding spices (such as the aniseed in the Spiced Grape Must, Raisin and Nut Cookies (see p 42) and the fennel in the *Schiacciata* (see p 170) it is perfect. You can, however, imitate the effect with the end of a rolling pin and a deep bowl.

Thermometer

Not absolutely necessary, and I have to admit I've never entered an Italian home which has one, and most things can be judged by eye, but if nervous when making custards, for example, it can be useful to know that the temperature must not go above 80°C (175°F).

Piping bags and nozzles

You can buy disposable piping bags in bulk very easily, in cookware shops and online, and I actually wash them and reuse them. You can buy non-disposable fabric ones too. They are good to have, and some of the more involved recipes require them so I'd urge you to keep some in your kitchen.

Melon baller

I'd almost argue for this to be on the necessary list, as these simple gadgets give me so much pleasure. Also known as a 'parisienne scoop' in rather more glamorous nomenclature, this small innocuous tool has many uses but has sadly fallen out of favour. It can be used to core apples or scrape the seeds from cucumbers, but most satisfyingly it can be used to make retro balls of sorbet or icy-cold melon.

Ice-cream machine

I couldn't say this is essential, but I highly recommend having one. If you like eating ice cream enough to want to make it yourself, and you enjoy being able to develop your own flavours, then it is definitely worth it. I've spent years pondering whether I could justify getting one and then finally did so for the purposes of this book, and I have used it at least twice a week since, even though I live within easy reach of excellent *gelaterie*. There are some reasonably priced ones, and the one I have also makes yoghurt. I put it into storage for the winter, and then bring it out in time for summer, a ritual that inspires me to start making ice cream again once the temperature rises.

Small paper cases

For housing the Marzipan Fruits (see p 225) and Salted Caramel Truffles (see p 226).

Food colouring

There is no end to the fun that can be had with food colouring. I have a set of 12 colours that I ordered inexpensively online. Children love playing about with it, and it makes cake decoration much more interesting. Essential for the Marzipan Fruits (see p 225).

Pasta machine

Not an essential, as anything you need to roll out you can do so using the old-fashioned method, a rolling pin and a board. However, it is rare to find an Italian kitchen without one of these, and they are extremely useful for the fast rolling of dough, especially for the Sunny Sardinian Citrus & Ricotta Tarts (see p 70).

RECIPE ADVICE

While I hope none of the recipes included here are too technical, there are certain rules in baking that have to be observed for things to turn out as you wish them to. I could never claim this book to be a baking bible or an exhaustive baking guide, but there are some processes and terms that I think are worth explaining, even if just for the sake of satisfying culinary curiosity. In most of the instances where things do get a bit scientific, I have attempted to explain things within the recipes and notes accompanying them. The following points are a little more general and, I hope, interesting and informative, arranged roughly in the order of the baking process.

Using a bain-marie (*bagnomaria*)

The bain-marie, double boiler, or *bagnomaria* as the Italians call it, is a simple system used for melting or gently heating and cooking ingredients. The name literally means 'Mary's bath' – a rather wonderful fact – and is named after Mary the Jewess, an ancient alchemist.

A bain-marie is achieved simply by placing a glass or metal bowl (these conduct heat best) over a saucepan of simmering water. The heat under the water should be medium and the bottom of the bowl should not be touching the water, otherwise the heat will be too strong. Using a bain-marie is the best way to melt chocolate (unless you like to do it in the microwave).

The term can also be used to describe the process of cooking delicate items such as flans in the oven in a roasting tin filled with hot water for gentle, even heat.

Melting white chocolate

When melting white chocolate it is important to make sure it is broken into small, even pieces, otherwise it will 'seize' – become lumpy and grainy. Melt it over a low heat, in a bain-marie. Don't stir it while it melts, but only once it has melted completely, and even then only a little. Either use chips or chop it into small even pieces using a sharp knife.

Seasoning with salt

I have explained why I add salt to most sweet things on page 248, but it is worth noting that a pinch of salt for me means a good pinch, not a few grains. I always taste my raw doughs, pastry, batters and gelatos for seasoning, the same way that I would a sauce or savoury dish.

Using a cartouche

A cartouche is a fancy word that describes a disc of greaseproof (waxed) paper or baking parchment that is used to cover the ingredients in a pan instead of a lid. The cartouche allows a little steam to escape but maintains a moist environment, preventing the substance being cooked drying out, as well as keeping it submerged and preventing a skin from forming on top.

Butter and butter creaming

When baking cakes, butter should always be at room temperature, which makes it much quicker and easier to cream with the sugar. Creaming butter and sugar is a way of incorporating air into cakes and creating a smooth batter. Cold butter will be harder to cream and the cake batter may split.

Cold butter is important in the recipes that call for the butter to be rubbed into the dough, as for crumble mixes or some pastries. Making pastry in a blender means the butter will soften anyway, and even if it becomes slightly warmer during mixing the pastry can be chilled afterwards.

Eggs

Eggs for baking should always be at room temperature. I keep one bowl of eggs outside the fridge for baking with, and one inside the fridge for keeping longer term and using in savoury dishes.

Whisking egg whites

Egg whites for whisking must contain absolutely no egg yolk, and the bowl and whisk must be clean and free of grease – otherwise the whites will not whisk properly. Whisk egg whites just until they hold smooth, soft peaks; don't overwhisk them until they look dry or grainy.

Folding ingredients together

Folding is a technical way of saying stirring very gently, using a large metal spoon, to incorporate an ingredient into cake batters without knocking out the air. It employs a swooping wrist motion, meaning you are stirring without beating or mixing, rather gently lifting and folding one thing into another, such as egg whites into a chocolate cake batter.

The 'sacrificial spoonful'

I love everything about this phrase and what it means. Something I learned at cooking school, it describes the process of folding egg whites into cake batters. When whisking egg whites for a cake batter, you are doing so to incorporate air into the finished cake. The air whipped into the whites can then be lost if you overmix the batter. In order to help incorporate the whipped whites into the batter you must first 'sacrifice' a large spoonful of the whites to lighten the batter and make it easier to incorporate the rest of the whites; the lighter your batter is, the easier it is to incorporate the fluffy whipped egg whites. So you stir in one spoonful relatively vigorously, sacrificing it to the batter, and this allows you to fold in the remaining whites very gently.

Custards and whisks

When making custards, particularly when cooking them out on the hob, many traditional recipes call for a wooden spoon to stir the mixture. I prefer to use a whisk (as I also do when making béchamel) as it gets to the edges of the pan more efficiently and generally stirs more evenly.

Using citrus fruit peel

When flavouring custards or panna cotta mixtures with citrus, I don't always finely grate the zest of the fruit; often a simple strip or two of peel is sufficient (and faster and easier than zesting). If you use a good swivel peeler these strips should contain very little of the white (bitter) pith and just the superficial zest.

Roasting nuts

Almost all nuts are better roasted. With the exceptions of the *Amaretti* (see p 34) and *Ricciolini* (see p 37), where the almond flavour is kept simple and fresh rather than toasty, most of the recipes here call for nuts to be roasted. The flavour of the nut is enhanced significantly by a quick roasting in the oven. I heat the oven to 170°C (340°F/Gas 3), spread them over the base of a baking sheet and roast them until they begin to smell good, 7–10 minutes. Allow them to cool before using.

Fats in baking

Sunflower and vegetable oil: Using flavourless oils such as sunflower, vegetable or groundnut adds little flavour to baked goods. It is instead a textural element that keeps them moist for longer, and gives a more moist crumb in general. Because butter adds so much flavour to the finished cake, it is necessary to compensate if using oil by adding strong flavours such as tangy yoghurt, spices or lots of zesty citrus.

Butter: Adds a delicious flavour and richness to cakes and a crispness to pastries and biscuits. Butter is solid at room temperature, so cakes made with butter tend to be a little less moist than those made with oil.

Lard: Makes pastries and biscuits more crisp, and its use is traditional in English and Italian baking, but it does have a flavour that some dislike. Lard in baking is covered in more detail on page 247.

Olive oil: A lovely ingredient in cakes and, as with sunflower or vegetable oil, makes cakes that stay moist for longer. A strong extra virgin olive oil can give a bitter flavour to a finished cake, however, and it is also a waste of a good oil that would probably be better used for dressing salads or for dipping bread into. For baking I tend to use a mildly flavoured extra virgin olive oil that is not too expensive.

Cooking until 'baveuse'

A fabulous French technical cooking term (another inheritance from cooking school days) which essentially means 'wobbly and a bit runny in the middle', like a good omelette or the best kind of baked custard. It derives from the French verb *baver* which means 'to drool or slobber'. It is the best description of the texture of the filling for the Citrus Curd Tart on page 52.

Resting and settling pastries

Most cakes, tarts and pastries need a good rest after they come out of the oven, so that they can settle and the texture can evolve as they cool. This is especially true for anything made with eggs.

Rising and proving dough

When letting yeasted dough rise, whether overnight in the fridge or at room temperature, it really *must* double in size. The more enrichment you add (such as spices, milk, butter and other fats, or eggs), the more slowly the yeast will work, and the longer you will have to leave the dough to rise and prove.

The rising or proving time (proving is the name of the second rise, which usually takes place after the item is shaped) will depend on the temperature of your kitchen and also on the yeast. Yeast is a living organism and as such is temperamental. The only sure way to know when the dough has risen and proved properly is when it has truly doubled in size. Once baked, the crumb will be much closer (less airy) if you do not allow the correct proving time. For the fluffiest brioches, buns and doughnuts, patience is key. Though most recipes say to prove for 45 minutes to 1 hour, brioche may take up to 2½ hours to prove properly, especially in an airy kitchen.

Overnight rising of enriched doughs: An easy way to make enriched doughs is to allow the dough to rise in the fridge overnight, so you only have to wait for it to prove the following day before you can bake and eat it. Beware, though, that the dough will take longer to come to room temperature and then to prove. You can shape the dough while it is still cold, but the yeast will only begin working after the dough comes up to room temperature, which may take 1–2 hours.

Doughs – the wetter the better: It follows that the wetter a bread or brioche dough is, the softer and moister the finished baked product will be too. However, wetter doughs are harder to work with, as they stick to everything around them. The doughs I have included here should be workable by hand, but are easiest worked by machine, which eliminates need to get sticky during kneading.

If you are working sticky doughs by hand, don't add lots of extra flour while kneading or shaping (a dusting on the baking sheet to prevent sticking is fine); using too much flour will change the consistency of the dough. Instead, lightly oil your work surface and put your bread scraper to good use.

Making sugar syrups and caramel: swirl, don't stir

Sugar syrup is simply a mixture of water and sugar. Never stir sugar syrup, which can cause crystals to form. Instead, pick up and swirl the pan gently to help the sugar dissolve. Do the same when making caramel. Even once the sugar begins to darken, do not stir it – just pick up the pan and keep swirling. Once you add butter and cream to the mixture, you can stir the caramel all you like.

Greasing and lining baking tins

I keep all my butter papers (just as my granny did) in the door of my fridge to use for greasing cake tins. Simply rub the inside of the tin with the butter paper, line it with baking parchment if you need to and it's ready.

Certain delicate cakes (such as *Pan di Spagna*, p 238) call for a greasing of butter and then a sprinkling of flour, which helps a drier cake to release. In this case, grease as normal with butter then sprinkle the flour over with a flick of your wrist. Pick up the tin and swirl to make sure the flour is distributed evenly and then tap out the excess.

Equally, as bundt tins and fancy tins cannot be lined with paper, they need to be buttered and floured to be sure the cake will release. Melt or soften a little butter and paint it into every bit of the tin using a pastry brush.

You can, if you wish, procure a 'baking spray', which sprays liquid oil into all the crevices of your cake tin.

Lining tart tins

Tart tins do not need to be greased, as pastry contains so much butter already. Once you have rolled out your pastry to the required thickness, flip it gently over your rolling pin and drape it over the tart case. Lift the sides and make sure to press dough down into the contours of the pan with your fingertips. Pass the rolling pin over the top of the case to gently cut off any overhang.

Moussing eggs: the ribbon trail

For certain recipes (such as *Pan di Spagna*, p 238) eggs need to be 'moussed'. This means whipping them until they are very pale and fluffy, and they form a ribbon trail – a trail of the whisked mixture which, when dangled from the end of the whisk, holds its ribbon shape for a few seconds. At this point you know the eggs are moussed sufficiently.

Rolling out pastry

Pastries with a high butter content (most of the sweet pastries included in this book) will become soft and begin to stick if the room temperature is warm. You can roll them between two pieces of baking parchment if things start to get difficult (or chill the pastry for a bit in the fridge).

Freezing

Leftover egg whites can be frozen, as can all pastries and biscuit doughs. Sadly, creams and custards can't.

Shaping buns

This is one of the most satisfying things in the world to do, but takes a little practice to get the knack. Shaping balls and buns out of dough is something I get endless pleasure from. I will attempt to explain the process here (there are also step-by-step photos, p 154). Once you have weighed out the dough, lightly oil your work surface. Take each ball of dough and make a claw shape with your hand to lightly cup the dough from above. Work the dough around and around inside your clawed hand until you have a smooth ball. Use the dough scraper to push and tuck the ball into smooth-domed perfection. Lift the ball lightly onto the prepared baking tray using a dough scraper.

Egg washing and glazing buns

Before baking buns and some tarts and pastries it is good to brush them with beaten egg to give them a shine and a lovely burnished colour. Any unused beaten egg can be used to make scrambled egg or given to the dog or cat – never thrown away! Brushing with milk is more economical but gives a much duller finish. Once they're baked and while still warm, you can brush the buns or brioche with mild runny honey to give a lovely shiny glaze. All buns looks better shiny.

Scalding milk

To bring milk, cream or a mixture of the two to a scald means to bring it, over heat, just to a simmer, until tiny bubbles appear at the edge of the pan. Boiling milk or cream will potentially cause them to split, become grainy or form a skin. For most recipes a mere scald is ample.

Slaking gelatine: This word can mean 'to quench or satisfy one's thirst' but in cookery terms it is the technical way of describing soaking gelatine leaves in cold water until they are soft. The term also means mixing cornflour with a little liquid until it forms a smooth paste, which can then be added to other liquids.

Upside-down cakes

I am a big fan of upside-down citrus cakes, which is why I have included them in both of my recipe books. The only problem is that people write to me saying theirs does not look like it does in the photo. To avoid any potential aesthetic disappointment, here are some tips:

- Citrus: Place the slices very close together in the base of the tin, just overlapping each other.
- After baking, once you have turned out the cake, it is inevitable that there will have been a little leakage of the batter through the slices of citrus fruit. You can brush this soft dough away using a pastry brush to show only the shiny fruit surface. Voila!

Macerating fruit

To macerate fruit means to squeeze fresh lemon juice and sprinkle a little sugar over prepared fruit, then let it sit until the fruit releases some of its juices and absorbs sweetness and acidity.

Strawberries benefit the most from macerating. Hulled, halved, then macerated in a little acidity and sugar, they taste more strawberry-ish than you could ever wish for; they become parodies of themselves. If your fruit is less than perfect, then this process is your saviour.

If your fruits are perfect, there may be no need to macerate them, but I often do it anyway because it gives you an instant, wonderfully sweet-sharp sauce too (no need to faff around making a syrup or compote).

There are some fruits that would be just plain wrong to macerate, like an apple (odd) or a melon (juicy enough on its own). Sub-par pears, peeled and sliced, macerate well, as do all berries, sliced fresh peaches, apricots, nectarines and plums.

In Italy, as good lemons are so readily available, it is common to spritz your fruit with some fresh lemon juice before eating, which is a habit I am happy to adopt.

To macerate fruit: Prepare your fruit (peel it, slice it, halve it or leave it whole, as required), put it in a bowl, squeeze over the juice of 1 lemon and sprinkle with 1–2 tablespoons of sugar. Leave the fruit, covered, for at least 10 minutes.

Crystallising leaves

A very simple way of decorating cakes, tarts and pastries (and a useful way of using up leftover egg whites) is to make crystallised leaves or rose petals. I like to use mint leaves, sage leaves, rose petals and lemon verbena leaves. Simply paint the (washed and dried) leaves with egg white using a pastry brush, then dip them in caster (superfine) sugar before leaving them on a rack to dry completely.

Serving ice cream and granita

It may perhaps be stating the obvious, but it's important to allow ice creams and sorbets to soften slightly before serving. When they are straight from the freezer the texture will be too icy and the flavour dulled. Remove them from the freezer 10–20 minutes before scooping.

Testing cakes for doneness

See a 'strand of spaghetti' on page 252. With thanks to both Nigella and Rachel Roddy for bringing this to my attention.

The only cake where this does not work is the Chocolate, Pear, Hazelnut & Brown Sugar Cake (see p 94), which I like to be a little gooey in the middle.

Soaking raisins

Raisins are tricky little devils in baking; they tend to burn quickly because of their high sugar content, and also to dry out. For this reason I soak them in liquid before using them, in orange juice, tea or alcohol.

Blanching almonds

If you prefer to buy whole almonds (they are cheaper and often better quality) then you can easily blanch them at home. Simply bring a saucepan of water to the boil, drop in the almonds and leave them for a minute or so until they bob to the surface. Fish them out and drain them, then pop off their skins with your fingers. Allow them to dry out again before using.

Seasoning sweet things

The best way to check if something sweet is going to be delicious is to taste the raw dough, mixture or batter. If it tastes delicious, then the finished product will taste delicious too. Most people taste savoury food for seasoning but very few taste their sweet mixes. These days a little raw egg is very unlikely to hurt you, and I would encourage you to taste all batters, doughs and cake or biscuit mixes to check for salt, acidity and sweetness. This way you can adjust accordingly by adding more lemon, orange juice or zest, salt or sugar. It is the only way to ensure it will taste the way you want it to.

A Glossy Glossary

I love words: the way they sound, their meanings and histories. Words say things, of course, but they are also images. The word 'orange', for example. It looks round. It sounds round. Your mouth is round when you say it. 'Doughnut' sounds like a big bite-ful, 'bun' like simple, plump joy.

Italian is truly a language of food. Almost every idiom, insult, exclamation and endearment is related in some way to eating or edibles. Children are affectionately called *patatino/patatina* (little potato), a common cuss is *cavolo* or 'cabbage', a reliable, generous person is a *pezzo di pane* (a piece of bread) and someone who has rose-tinted spectacles is described as having *prosciutto sugli occhi*, or 'ham in their eyes'.

Living in Italy I have been forced to learn another language (somewhat imperfectly), and in learning it I have discovered many new, favourite words. As the language I deal in is predominantly that of food, I have fallen for many Italian words that correspond to eating and seem to be especially evocative. Here are some of them, for pleasure and maybe even for practice, for the next time you are in Italy and feel the need to bite into something *croccante*, or to squish a bun, bread roll or doughnut between your fingers and say – with a little sigh – the word that captures the sensation.

Burrosa: This literally means 'buttery', and describes many baked English things which are undeniably buttery in their make-up. It is also often used to describe voluptuous Rubenesque women which I think is pleasantly evocative. 'Buttery-ness' in every way appeals to me.

Cremosa: Creamy, but in a creamier way, like gelato.

Croccante: Crunchy. Again, it sounds how it is.

Crostata: A tart. Confusingly a *torta* is a cake, not a tart, though it sounds like it should be the reverse. The 'crosta' is a crust, so a *crostata* literally describes the pastry crust of a tart.

Friabile: Crumbly, but in a sort of flaky way, like very good pastry. It combines words that we would use in English, like short, flaky, crumbly, into one highly descriptive word. It sounds like it feels. Before writing this book I'd never heard of the equivalent in English, friable, which means 'easily crumbled', and is an irresistible phrase in itself.

Imburrare: To grease, or to 'inbutter'. Perhaps it's my obsession with butter, but something about the idea of 'inbuttering' things makes me very happy. To 'grease' something sounds much more mechanical and prosaic in comparison.

Inzuppare: Literally translated as 'to in-soup' – or to soak something in liquid. As you would a biscuit in a cup of tea, a crust of bread in a bowl of soup, or the *tuppo* from your brioche in the melting puddle of your gelato.

Leggero: Light. This is used to describe both cakes and situations, and is (obviously) the antonym of *pesante*. I'm sure we all often wish that our cakes, and our lives in general, could always be *leggero*.

Morbida: Morbida means 'soft', but in a gently-smooth, less squishy way. There is a shop in my local town, only for women, which is called *Bella Morbida*, which means, literally, 'beautiful soft'.

Morbidissima: Very, very soft/smooth. See *sofficissima*.

Pesante: Pronounced *pes-ant-ay*. This literally translates as 'heavy', and is the word to use for (failed) cakes. It is also used metaphorically, to describe a situation, person or attitude. Sadly, it doesn't really have an accurate equivalent in English which is a shame because it is an extremely useful way of describing things. People can be *pesante*, tasks can be *pesante*, life is all-too-often *pesante*. It sort of means arduous, long-winded, gratuitously heavy.

Schiacciata: Pronounced *ski-atch-ata* squashed, like the grape bread on page 170. Another of my favourite examples of onomatopoeia.

Soffice: Pure onomatopoeia. Pronounced *soff-e-chay,* this is the appropriate word for the bread/bun/doughnut squishing moment. *Soffice* means soft, but in a specific way especially applicable to tactile objects. People are not *soffice*, for example, but cakes and buns are.

Sofficissima: There is a wonderful grammatical rule in Italian which allows you to create dramatic descriptive words simply by adding *-issima* onto the end of an adjective. *Bellissima*, thus, is 'very beautiful', but whilst the English 'very' sounds strangely dry and cold, the Italian *-issima* sounds suitably effusive. *Sofficissima*, thus, means 'very soft', but in a more exquisitely soft, Italian way.

Index

A

B

C

D

E

F

G

H

I

J

L

M

N

O

P

R

S

T

V

W

Y

Z

Acknowledgements

I must be honest and say that this book was a giant leap of faith for many reasons. Writing it – and shooting it – during a global pandemic was not something I ever envisaged. The only reason it is here now, being held in your hands, is thanks to the tireless hard work and unshakeable faith of so many brilliant people.

Firstly to my mum. Her passion for biscuits, butter and sugar inspired me from the very beginning. Her unflinching positivity and support throughout the whole process has been invaluable and her own creativity with cake decoration and marzipan when we were children was, and continues to be, a huge inspiration. She tested recipes for me, wilfully changed them (like me she is incapable of following them) and thus gave me totally hopeless feedback, but always with a string of whatsapped 'yums' of appreciation, which is all I really needed to hear, as – knowing her as I know myself – I tested the recipes again myself anyway, just to be sure.

To my dad, for cooking a different dish from my first book, *Bitter Honey*, every night of the week, and for keeping me sane during a long lockdown by sending me daily updates on the weather in England, his diet and the state of the garden.

To my older brother, Christopher, for tasting half of the recipes, and being only half as critical as I am.

To my younger brother, Billy, for trying and failing to make *Seadas*, and for his support.

To Charlotte Bland, for being the most exquisite photographer: uncompromising, subtle, delicate and with an extraordinary eye for beauty and detail. For believing in the project and for loving Sardinia, fruit, shadows and cats as much as I do.

To Sylvia Black, for her help with Sardinian recipes and stories, and her *Sbriciolona*.

To Holly Peters, for appearing as if by magic, and becoming an integral part in the making of this book. For hilarious stories, sheep videos and boundless enthusiasm.

To Kajal Mistry, for being my brilliant and upbeat Publisher, for believing in the book from the beginning, and for allowing me to write four pages of pure, self-indulgent fruit worship.

To my agent, Anne Kibel, for taking on the book from the word go with plenty of enthusiasm.

To Tamara Vos, for her brilliant styling, love of all things squishy and for custard and kitchen prowess.

To the Two Tiny Cats, for not giving a damn about anything going on around them, unless it involved custard.

To my grandmother, always, who inspired in me a lifelong love of coffee, cats, cakes and cream, of Italy and Edward Lear, and almost everything that I still love today.

To Rose Ashby, for celebrating with me even before I knew there was anything to celebrate.

To Harriet Piercy, for putting me up and putting up with me.

To Allegra Pomilio, for sending me a box of wonderful crockery, which then became the most brilliant props.

To Victoria Green, for edits and encouragement.

To Francesca Bruzzese, for making the *maritozzi* and for general encouragement.

To Domu Antiga and the Lai family, for their hospitality.

To Giulia Lai, for her lovely breakfasts, her eye for beauty and her knowledge of delicious *dolci*.

To Simona Fenari, for keeping me sane during the long and lonely lockdown months.

To Loredana Fenari, for being *un pezzo di pane*, and for scolding me constantly.

To Monica Putzolu, for her help, generosity and advice.

Huge and heartfelt thanks especially to Mauro Mastinu, for his invaluable help with translation and his Sardinian stories: *che vita triste senza lo strutto! Grazie mille.*

To Gabriele Sanna, for Alfonso Bialetti.

To Andrew Graves, for showing me where to buy candied fruit, introducing me to so many of the books which are in the bibliography, and for showing me the best places to eat gelato in Cagliari.

To Stroma Sinclair, for her feedback and help.

To Alyson Parkes, for her invaluable help with recipe testing.

To Susan Low, for being an excellent and committed editor, and for much-appreciated words of encouragement.

To Eve Marleau, for her positivity and careful eye.

To Evi-O studio for their brilliant and beautiful design and illustrations.

To Emiko Davies, for her lovely recipe for Rosemary *Fior di Latte*.

To the one-and-only Luca Vacca: for his contagious *brio*, for *Bomboloni* for breakfast, and for *Besciamella*.

Bibliography
or for further reading

Though they're not technically the same thing, a bibliography being a list of books studied and 'further reading' a list of books recommended for study, I nevertheless wanted to include a list combining the two because any books I read, saw or found useful in the process of writing this book are most definitely worth seeking out.

I wrote in my first book, *Bitter Honey*, that cooking is a magpie business (a quote I stole from the great Fay Maschler), by which I mean we see something shiny and we seize upon it; we may change and adapt it, we may accessorise our nests with it and make it our 'own', but ultimately we recipe-writers are collectors and curators as well as creators. For this reason it is important to give credit where credit is due. This book is by no means as encyclopaedic in scope as I would have wished it to be (in a perfect world without deadlines), so it cannot fail to be a good thing to suggest a number of other titles that fill in the (many) gaps.

1. Atlee, Helena. 2014. *The Land where the Lemons Grow*. London: Penguin
2. Artusi, Pellegrino. 1970. *La Scienza in Cucina e L'Arte di Mangiar Bene*. Turin: Einaudi
3. Costantino, Rosetta. 2013. *Southern Italian Desserts*. New York: Ten Speed Press
4. David, Elizabeth. 2006. *Italian Food*. London: The Folio Society (my favourite edition because of the beautiful illustrations by Sophie MacCarthy)
5. Davies, Emiko. 2016. *Florentine*. Australia: Hardie Grant
6. Del Conte, Anna. 1993. *I Dolci: Sweet Things*. New York: Simon & Schuster
7. _____ 2013. *The Gastronomy of Italy*. London: Pavilion
8. *Dolci di Sardegna*. 2010. Sardinia: Edizione della Torre
9. Field, Carol. 1985. *The Italian Baker*. New York: Ten Speed Press
10. Fort, Matthew. 2008. *Sweet Honey, Bitter Lemons*. London: Ebury
11. Goldstein, Darra. 2015. *The Oxford Companion to Sugar and Sweets*. Oxford: Oxford University Press
12. Gray, Rose and Ruth Rogers. 2009. *The River Café Classic Italian Cookbook*. London: Penguin
13. Grigson, Jane. 1982. *Jane Grigson's Fruit Book*. London: Penguin
14. Kenedy, Jacob. 2011. *Bocca: Cookbook*. London: Bloomsbury
15. Lawson, Nigella. 2012. *Nigellissima*. London: Chatto & Windus
16. Liddell, Caroline and Robin Weir. 1995. *Frozen Desserts*. London: Grub Street
17. Locatelli, Giorgio. 2006. *Made in Italy: Food and Stories*. London: Fourth Estate
18. _____2011. *Made in Sicily*. London: Fourth Estate
19. Loren, Sophia. 1998. *Recipes & Memories*. New York: GT Publishing
20. Riley, Gillian. 2007. *The Oxford Companion to Italian Food*. Oxford: Oxford University Press
21. Roddy, Rachel. 2017. *Two Kitchens: Family Recipes from Sicily and Rome*. London: Headline
22. Roden, Claudia. 2014. *The Food of Italy*. London: Square Peg
23. Simeti, Mary Taylor. 1986. *On Persephone's Island, A Sicilian Journal*. London: Penguin
24. ____ 1991. *Pomp and Sustenance, Twenty-Five Centuries of Sicilian Food*. New York: Henry Holt
25. ____ and Mary Grammatico. 1994. *Bitter Almonds*. London: Bantam
26. Travers, Kitty. 2018. *La Grotta Ices*. London: Square Peg

Quadrille, Penguin Random House UK,
One Embassy Gardens, 8 Viaduct Gardens,
London SW11 7BW

Quadrille Publishing Limited is part of the Penguin Random House group of companies whose addresses can be found at global.penguinrandomhouse.com

First published by Hardie Grant Books in 2021

www.penguin.co.uk

A CIP catalogue record for this book is available from the British Library

ISBN: 978-1-78488-422-2
10 9 8 7

Publisher and Commissioner: Kajal Mistry
Editor: Eve Marleau
Design and Illustrations: Evi-O.Studio | Susan Le
Photographer: Charlotte Bland,
except for image on p 143 © Matt Russell
Food Stylist: Tamara Vos and Letitia Clark
Kitchen Assistant: Holly Peters
Prop Stylist: Letitia Clark and Charlotte Bland
Recipe-editor: Susan Low
Proofreader: Caroline West
Indexer: Vanessa Bird
Production Controller: Nikolaus Ginelli

Colour reproduction by p2d
Printed in China by C&C Offset Printing Co., Ltd.

The authorised representative in the EEA is Penguin Random House Ireland, Morrison Chambers, 32 Nassau Street, Dublin D02 YH68.

Penguin Random House is committed to a sustainable future for our business, our readers and our planet. This book is made from Forest Stewardship Council® certified paper.

FSC
www.fsc.org
MIX
Paper | Supporting responsible forestry
FSC® C018179

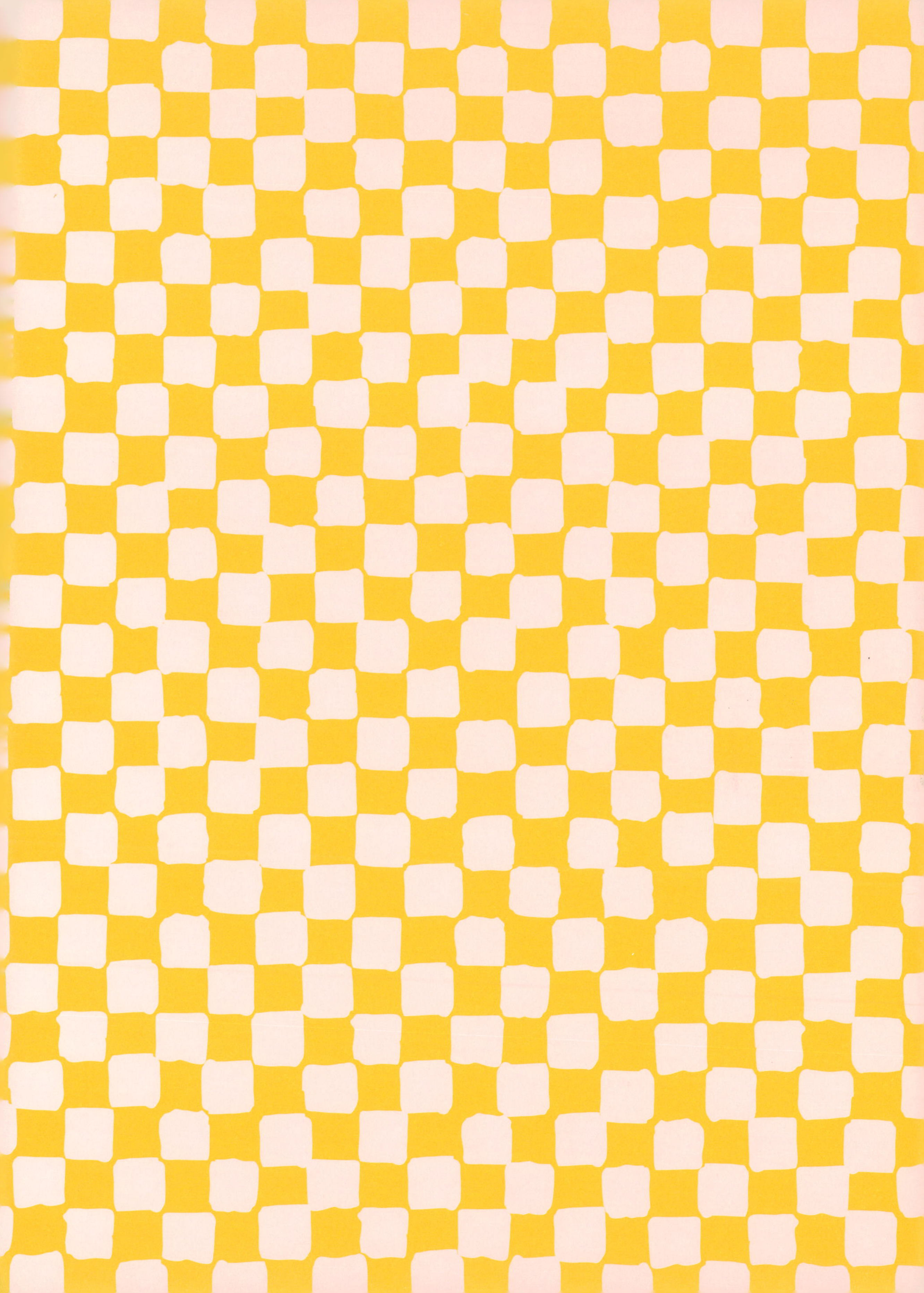